BOTH SIDES OF

Both sides of the Border

From Chester to Chepstow

An Anthology of writing on the Welsh Border Region

Dewi Roberts

In memory of my parents
Emlyn and Margaret Roberts, border people.

ISBN: 0-86381-461-1

Cover: Smala

First published in 1998 by Gwasg Carreg Gwalch,
12 Iard yr Orsaf, Llanrwst, Conwy, Wales.

☎ *(01492) 642031*

Printed and Published in Wales

Contents

Introduction

Over the centuries the border region between Wales and England has been the scene of violent conflict and skirmishing. It is hardly surprising that the consciousness of the past is so strong here, and that this should have inspired writers of all kinds: early travellers, historians, diarists and novelists and poets. This is the first time that an anthology focusing on the region has included all these genres of writing, for previous selections have tended to confine themselves to poetry.

The reign of Offa and the construction of the Dyke, the Roman invasion and the last stand of Caractacus, the attempted subjugation of Wales by Henry II, the revolt of Owain Glyndŵr and the supremacy of the Marcher Lordships are among the historical topics covered from a selection of varied sources.

Poets and novelists, including A.E. Housman and Mary Webb, have found creative stimulas here and their writings have a great deal to tell us about the border experience.

This experience has many manifestations, but central to it is the Welsh consciousness of the threatening near proximity of a larger, colonising country with a wholly different historic, linguistic and cultural heritage. A.E. Housman's powerful *The Welsh Marches* deals more memorably with this area of experience, with its origins in bloody conflict, than any other poem I know.

Even in the nineteenth century, from an English perspective the marcher country still suggested danger and a sense of the unknown, and this also is reflected in literature. When George Borrow was in Llangollen in 1854 he spoke to a local man who appeared to enjoy telling him how the English and the Welsh dealt with those unfortunate enough to be caught after crossing Offa's Dyke

> ' . . . there was a time when it was customary for the English to cut off the ears of every Welshman who was found to the east of Offa's Dyke, and for the Welsh to hang every Englishman whom they found to the west of it'.

Even now, as we approach the millennium, these ancient memories live on, although nowadays the border region is much more benign, and the entire geographical expanse has been opened up for the benefit of the tourist. Now you can drive from Chester to Chepstow in half a day, while three or four days of energetic walking will enable you to walk the length of Offa's Dyke.

With this in mind, I have arranged the material in this selection in the form of an itinerary which will take the reader on a journey from the North to the South. It is important to see the borders in a cohesive way, as a unique geographical part of the British Isles in its own right.

I have drawn on the work of English writers from the last four centuries, but have also included translations from the works of certain Welsh language writers, including two complete short stories by Islwyn Ffowc Ellis and R. Gerallt Jones. Mr Jones' 'The Letter' encapsulates the experience of crossing borders superbly in this tale of a boy from Llŷn who is sent to a public school in Shrewsbury.

On a personal note, I have some border blood in my own veins, for both my late parents came from the Montgomeryshire border region, and it was on a farm quite close to Llanfyllin that I spent some fondly remembered childhood holidays.

Let me end with a favourite anecdote, once related to me by my father. Many years ago a farmer died while working in his fields and his body collapsed directly across the border-line dividing Montgomeryshire and Shropshire. This singular situation posed the problem of which country he should be buried in. This was earnestly discussed by his friends and acquaintances, but they failed to reach an agreement. But then a wise man said: 'Let's bury him where his heart is'.

Well, I know where my heart lies.

Dewi Roberts

Acknowledgements

Both the publisher and the editor wish to thank the following for allowing their work to be included in the book:

Bryan Martin Davies for permission to include translations of two of his poems, and to Grahame Davies for translating these especially for this book; R. Gerallt Jones for his short story 'The Letter', which originally appeared in 'Twenty Five Welsh Short Stories' edited by Gwyn Jones and Islwyn Ffowc Ellis and published by the Oxford University Press.

Islwyn Ffowc Ellis for his short story 'Black Barren', which originally appeared in 'The Penguin Book of Short Stories' edited by Alun Richards; Tim Liardet for 'Balloonists Over Oswestry' which was specially commissioned; Andrew Sumner for 'Chester Cathedral'.

Gladys Mary Coles for the poems 'The Kingdom of Sphagnum', 'On Offa's Dyke', and 'Bomere, Shropshire'.

Margery Lea for 'In the Border Mountain'.

University of Wales Press for a passage from 'John Wesley in Wales' edited by A.H. Williams.

Professors William Tydeman and Alun Jones for passages from 'A Pedestrian Tour of North Wales' by Joseph Hucks.

J.M. Dent for an extract from 'Tramping Through Wales' by John Moore (1931); Wrexham Borough Council for a passage from 'A History of Wrexham' edited by A.H. Dodd.

Patricia V. Dawson for 'Sight Seeing' from 'The Kiln' published by Hub Editions; Random House UK Limited for the passage from Francis Kilvert's Diary; Gee and Son (Denbigh) Ltd for extracts from: 'My Dad's the Village Blacksmith' by Alf Strange, 'Flintshire from Earliest Times to the Act of Union' edited by C.R. Williams and 'Michael Farraday in Wales' edited by Dafydd Tomos. Reproduced by permission of Penguin Books Ltd, an extract from 'The Annals of Imperial Rome' by Tacitus in the translation by Michael Grant.

John Idris Jones for 'Berwyn Christmas'.

The Society of Authors as the Literary Representative of the Estate of A.E. Housman 'The Welsh Marches' by A.E. Housman.

Denbighshire Record Office for extracts from the diary of Askew Roberts.

Grahame Davies for his translations of two of his poems.

On The Border

They were all charm.
A polished pair
from the posh side
of Gloucestershire.

He bought me a drink
and spoke of his son
an officer type
in some damned regiment.
'I'm so awfully
proud of him, y'know.'

They were going to Rhaeadr
which she pronounced RADA
as if it were some bloody acting school
then on to Pembrokeshire
which they thought would be quite quaint.

'You know, there's a bleeding tree at Nevern,
a tree that actually bleeds.'
She looked at me, eager for response.
'They say it will go on bleeding
till the Welsh get their own prince.
They'll have to wait a long time, won't they?'
She laughed a well-bred little laugh.
'I don't know,' I said,
'We're working on it.'
She did a double take. 'Oh. You're Welsh?'

Herbert Williams

'An Indescribable Old Town'

The great nineteenth century novelist Nathaniel Hawthorne was, from 1853 until 1857 the American Consul in Liverpool and during this period he kept an extensive journal in which he recorded in some detail visits to both North Wales and the northern border region. Here we find him in Chester.

> October 1st, 1853. On Thursday I went with Mr Ticknor to Chester by railway. It is quite an indescribable old town, and I feel at last as if I had had a glimpse of old England. The wall encloses a large space within the town, but there are numerous houses and streets not included within its precincts. Some of the principal streets pass under the ancient gateways; and at the side there are flights of steps, giving access to the summit. Around the top of the whole wall, a circuit of about two miles, there runs a walk, well paved with flagstones, and broad enough for three persons to walk abreast. On one side – that towards the country – there is a parapet of red freestone, three or four feet high. On the other side there are houses, rising up immediately from the wall, so that they seem a part of it. The height of it, I suppose, may be thirty or forty feet, and, in some parts, you look down from the parapet into orchards, where there are tall apple-trees, and men on the branches, gathering fruit, and women and children among the grass, filling bags or baskets. There are prospects of the surrounding country among the buildings outside the wall; at one point, a view of the river Dee, with an old bridge of arches. It is all very strange, very quaint, very curious to see how the town has overflowed its barrier, and how, like many institutions here, the ancient wall still exists, but is turned to quite another purpose than what it was meant for – so far as it serves any purpose at all. There are three or four towers in the course of the circuit; the most interesting being one from the top of which King Charles I is said to have seen the rout of his army by the Parliamentarians. We ascended the short flight of steps that led up into the tower, where an old man pointed out the site of the battle-field, now thickly studded with buildings, and told us what we had already learned from the guidebook. After this we went into the cathedral, which I will perhaps describe on some other occasion, when I shall have seen more of it, and to better advantage. The cloisters gave us the strongest impression of antiquity; the stone arches being so worn and blackened by time. Still an American must always have imagined a better cathedral than this. There were some immense windows of painted

glass, but all modern. In the chapter-house we found a coal fire burning in a grate, and a large heap of old books – the library of the cathedral – in a discreditable state of decay – mildewed, rotten, neglected for years. The sexton told us that they were to be arranged and better ordered. Over the door, inside, hung two faded and tattered banners, being those of the Cheshire regiment.

The most utterly indescribable feature of Chester is the Rows, which every traveller has attempted to describe. At the height of several feet above some of the oldest streets, a walk runs through the front of the houses, which project over it. Back off the walk there are shops; on the outer side is a space of two or three yards, where the shopmen place their tables, and stands, and show-cases; overhead, just high enough for persons to stand erect, a ceiling. At frequent intervals little narrow passages go winding in among the houses, which all along are closely conjoined, and seem to have no access or exit, except through the shops, or into these narrow passages, where you can touch each side with your elbows, and the top with your hand. We penetrated into one or two of them, and they smelt anciently and disagreeably. At one of the doors stood a pale-looking, but cheerful and good-natured woman, who told us that she had come to that house when first married, twenty-one years before, and had lived there ever since; and that she felt as if she had been buried through the best years of her life. She allowed us to peep into her kitchen and parlour, – small, dingy, dismal, but yet not wholly destitute of a home look. She said that she had seen two or three coffins in a day, during cholera times, carried out of that narrow passage into which her door opened. These avenues put me in mind of those which run through ant-hills, or those which a mole makes underground.

Nathaniel Hawthorne (1804-1864)
from 'Passages from the English Notebooks'

Poetic Wrath

Upon the walls it is possible to make the whole compass of the city, there being a good but narrow walk upon them. The northern wall abuts upon a frightful ravine, at the bottom of which is a canal. From the western one there is a noble view of the Welsh hills.

As I stood gazing upon the hills from the wall a ragged man came up and asked for charity.

'Can you tell me the name of that tall hill?' said I, pointing in the direction of the south-west. 'That hill, sir,' said the beggar, 'is called Moel Vamagh; I ought to know something about it as I was born at its foot.' 'Moel,' said I, 'a bald hill; Vamagh, maternal or motherly. Moel Vamagh, the Mother Moel.' 'Just so, sir,' said the beggar' 'I see you are a Welshman, like myself, though I suppose you come from the South – Moel Vamagh is the mother Moel, and is called so because it is the highest of all the Moels.' 'Did you ever hear of a place called Mold?' said I. 'Oh, yes, your honour,' said the beggar; 'many a time; and many's the time I have been there.' 'In which direction does it lie?' said I. 'Towards Moel Vamagh, your honour,' said the beggar, 'which is a few miles beyond it; you can't see it from here, but look towards Moel Vamagh and you will see over it.' 'Thank you,' said I, and gave something to the beggar, who departed, after first taking off his hat. Long and fixedly did I gaze in the direction of Mold. The reason which induced me to do so was the knowledge of an appalling tragedy transacted there in the old time, in which there is every reason to suppose a certain Welsh bard, called Lewis Glyn Cothi, had a share.

This man, who was a native of South Wales, flourished during the wars of the Roses. Besides being a poetical he was something of a military genius, and had a command of foot in the army of the Lancastrian Jasper Earl of Pembroke, the son of Owen Tudor, and half-brother of Henry the Sixth. After the battle of Mortimer's Cross, in which the Earl's forces were defeated, the warrior bard found his way to Chester, where he married the widow of a citizen and opened a shop, without asking the permission of the mayor, who with the officers of justice came and seized all his goods, which, according to his own account, filled nine sacks, and then drove him out of the town. The bard in a great fury indited an awdl, in which he invites Reinallt ap Gruffydd ap Bleddyn, a kind of predatory chieftain, who resided a little way off in Flintshire, to come and set the town on fire, and slaughter the inhabitants, in revenge for the wrongs he had suffered, and then proceeds to vent all kinds of imprecations against the mayor and people of Chester, wishing, amongst other things, that they might soon hear that the Dee had become too shallow to bear their ships – that a certain cutaneous disorder might attack the wrists of great and small, old and young, laity and clergy – that grass might grow in their streets – that Ilar and Cyveilach, Welsh saints, might slay them – that dogs might snarl at them – and that the king of heaven, with the saints Brynach and Non, might afflict them with blindness – which piece, however ineffectual in inducing God and the saints to visit the Chester people with the curses with which the furious bard wished them to be afflicted, seems to have produced somewhat of its intended effect on the chieftain, who shortly afterwards, on learning that the mayor and many of the Chester people were present at the fair of Mold, near which place he resided, set upon them at the head of his forces, and after a desperate combat, in which many lives were lost, took the mayor prisoner, and drove those of his people who survived into a tower, which he set on fire and burnt, with all the unhappy wretches which it contained, completing the horrors of the day by hanging the unfortunate mayor.

Conversant as I was with all this strange history, is it wonderful that I looked with great interest from the wall of Chester in the direction of Mold?

George Borrow: 'Wild Wales' (1862) (1803-1881)

Chester Cathedral

Imprinted in glowing sandstone
Is a tale of fossil tides
And cyclic seasons
In this English shire.

Pity cold monks,
Their labours lit by winter-light
In this place of rock
Among river-damp and sodden clay.
Pity soldiers
Whose bloodied colours hang corpse-grey
Among cold vaulting stone,
But whose bodies lie beyond the pale
Of this, their sap-green county.

But stone-hard and ages dirty,
This cathedral draws
A joyful song of faith
From craftsmen who made their lives
A statement of one certainty.

We, the pilgrims,
Walk in cloistered light –
A zebra-shade
From a filigree of stone
In the warm sanctity
Of a silent summer evening.

Andrew Sumner (1993)

The Torturous Wall

Henry James was an American novelist with a passion for European culture. This eventually resulted in him moving permanently to live in England, and in his novel, 'The Ambassadors' we find him writing of a town located very close to the Welsh border, Chester.

> The torturous wall – girdle, long since snapped, of the little swollen city, half held in place by careful civic hands – wanders in narrow file between parapets smoothed by peaceful generations, pausing here and there for a dismantled gate or a bridged gap, with rises and drops,

steps up and steps down, queer twists, queer contacts, peeps into homely streets and under the brows of gables, views of cathedral tower and waterside fields, of huddled English town and ordered English country. Too deep almost for words was the delight of these things to Strether; yet as deeply mixed with it were certain images of his inward picture. He had trod this walk in the far-off time, at twenty-five; but that, instead of spoiling it, only enriched it for present feeling and marked his renewal as a thing substantial enough to share.

They had stopped, in the afternoon sunshine – constantly pausing, in their stroll, for the sharper sense of what they saw – and Strether rested on one of the high sides of the old stony groove of the little rampart. He leaned back on this support with his face to the tower of the cathedral, now admirably commanded by their station, the high red-brown mass, square and subordinately spired and crocketed, retouched and restored, but charming to his long-sealed eyes and with the first swallows of the year weaving their flight all round it.

Henry James: (1843-1916) from 'The Ambassadors'

Early Skirmishing

In 1157 King Henry II made preparations for his first Welsh war. The domestic quarrels of the Welsh princes furnished him with an excellent pretext. Cadwaladr appealed to Henry against his relatives, and, of course, found a gracious reception. Orders were issued for an expedition into North Wales. The invasion was two-fold – by land and sea. The host assembled near Chester, on Saltney Marsh, and was joined by Madog, prince of Powys. Owen Gwynedd, with his three sons and all his forces, entrenched himself at Basingwerk. The King himself set off by the sea coast, hoping to fall upon the Welsh all unawares. Owen's sons, however, were on the watch, and in the narrow pass of Consilt the English suddenly found themselves face to face with the foe. Entangled in the woody, marshy ground, they were easily routed by the nimble, light-armed Welsh, and the cry that the king himself had fallen caused the constable, Henry of Essex, to drop the royal standard and fly in despair. Owen, however, thought it prudent to withdraw from Basingwerk, and seek a more inaccessible retreat. Henry pushed on to Rhuddlan, and there fortified the castle. Meanwhile, the fleet had sailed under the command of Madog ap Meredith. It touched at Anglesey, and there landed a few troops, whose sacrilegious behaviour brought upon them such vengeance from the outraged islanders that their terrified comrades sailed back at once to Chester, where they learned that the war was ended.

Thomas Stephens: 'Welshmen' (1901)

Grahame Davies was born and brought up in Coedpoeth and is now a journalist working in South Wales. He has published widely in Welsh-language magazines and his first collection of poems 'Adennill Tir' was published in 1997.

Liverpool

When I was a lad up in Flintshire,
a day to remember for me
was to take a trip over the border
to the city at the edge of the sea.

With her white towers on the horizon
the world seemed to bow at her feet,
and we felt a pride in her accent
as we eavesdropped her talk in the street.

But now, those same Merseyside voices
are no more the sign of a spree.
I don't need to travel to Liverpool
when Liverpool's travelled to me.

Grahame Davies. Translated by the poet (1997)

The Dee's Singularity

Next after the Thames and the Severn, no river in this country can be named that is more worthy. The Dee has this double claim on our attention, that it is both a Welsh stream and an English stream. It possesses to the full the interest which belongs to every border-region.

The Dee has been, to a singular extent, a favourite with the English Poets: and this in reference to one peculiar characteristic which is supposed to belong to it. Whether it be from some reminiscence of the Druids, or from whatever cause, the 'holiness' of this 'wizard stream' meets us at every turn: so that a sacred mystery seems to brood over its waters, which belongs to no other stream in England.

J.S. Howson: 'The River Dee' (1892)

Fortelling the Future

A brook that was suppos'd much business to have seen
Which had an ancient bound 'twixt Wales and England been,
And noted was by both to be an ominous flood,
That, changing of his fords, the future ill or good
Of either country told, of either's war or peace,
The sickness or the health, the dearth or the increase.'

Michael Drayton (1563-1631) from 'Poly-Olbion'

The Veteran Angler

Although not a great writer Washington Irving managed to bring a fresh eye to everything he wrote about. He spent many years away from America and part of this period was spent in England and Scotland. He also visited the Welsh border region on at least one occasion, and here we find him on the banks of the River Alyn near Rossett.

In a morning stroll along the banks of the Alyn, a beautiful little stream which flows down from the Welsh hills and throws itself into the Dee, my attention was attracted to a group seated on the margin. On approaching I found it to consist of a veteran angler and two rustic disciples. The former was an old fellow, with a wooden leg, with clothes very well but very carefully patched, betokening poverty, honestly come by, and decently maintained. His face bore the marks of former storms, but present fair weather; its furrows had been worn into a habitual smile; his iron-grey locks hung about his ears, and he had altogether the good humoured air of a constitutional philosopher who was disposed to take the world as it went . . .

The old man was busy in examining the maw of a trout which he had just killed, to discover by the contents which insects were seasonable for bait; and was lecturing to his companions, who appeared to listen with infinite deference.

I could not but remark the gallant manner in which the veteran angler stumped from one part of the brook to another; waving his rod in the air, to keep the line from dragging on the ground, or catching among the bushes; and the adroitness with which he would throw his fly to any particular place; sometimes swimming it along a little rapid; sometimes casting it into one of those dark holes made by a twisted root or overhanging bank in which the large trout are apt to lurk. In the meantime he was giving instructions to his two disciples: showing them the manner in which they should handle their rods, fix their flies, and play them along the surface of the stream.

It was part of the great plain of Cheshire, close by the beautiful vale of Gresford, and just where the inferior Welsh hills begin to swell up from fresh-smelling meadows. The day, too, like that recorded in Walton's great work, was mild and sunshiny, with now and then a soft-dropping shower that sowed the whole earth with diamonds.

I fell into conversation with the old angler and was so much entertained that, under pretext of receiving instructions in his art, I kept company with him almost the whole day; wandering along the banks of the stream, and listening to his talk. He was very communicative, having all the easy garrulity of cheerful old age; and I fancy was a little flattered by having an opportunity of displaying his piscatorial lore; for who does not like now and then to play the sage?

He had been much of a rambler in his day, and had passed some years of his youth in America, particularly in Savannah, where he had entered into trade, and had been ruined by the indiscretion of a partner. He had afterwards experienced many ups and downs in life, until he got into the navy, where his leg was carried away by a cannon ball at the Battle of Camperdown.

This was the only stroke of real good fortune he had ever experienced, for it got him a pension which together with some small paternal property brought him in a revenue of nearly forty pounds. On this he retired to his native village, where he lived quietly and independently, and devoted the remainder of his life to 'the noble art of angling'.

I found that he had read Izaak Walton attentively, and he seemed to have imbibed all his simple frankness and prevalent good humour.

On parting with the old angler I inquired after his place of abode, and, happening to be in the neighbourhood of the village a few days afterwards, I had the curiosity to seek him out. I found him living in an old cottage, containing only one room, but a perfect curiosity in its method and arrangement. I was on the skirts of the village, on a green bank, a little back from the road, with a small garden in front, stocked with kitchen herbs and adorned with a few flowers. The whole front of the cottage was overrun with a honeysuckle. On the top was a ship for a weathercock. The interior was filled up in a truly nautical style, his ideas of comfort and convenience having been acquired on the berth-deck of a man-of-war . . . . His implements for angling were carefully disposed on nails and hooks about the room. On a shelf was arranged his library, containing a work on angling, much worn, a Bible covered with canvas, an old volume or two of voyages, a nautical almanac and a book of songs.

I found him seated on a bench before the door smoking his pipe in the soft evening sunshine. His cat was purring soberly on the threshold, and his parrot describing some strange evolutions in an iron ring, that swung in the centre of his cage. He had been angling all day, and gave me a history of his sport with as much minuteness as a general would talk over a campaign, being particularly animated in relating the manner in which he had taken a large trout, which had completely tasked all his skill and wariness, and which he had sent as a trophy to mine hostess of the inn.

The whole tenor of his life was quiet and inoffensive, being principally passed about the neighbouring streams, when the weather and season were favourable; and at other times he employed himself at home, preparing his fishing tackle for the next campaign, or manufacturing rods, nets, and floes for his patrons and pupils among the gentry.

Washington Irving (1783-1859) from 'The Sketch Book'

A Lovely Little Seclusion

Those parts, indeed, of Flintshire, or even of Denbighshire, which lay near to Chester, were not in any very eminent sense attractive. The vale of Gressford, for instance, within the Flintshire border, and yet not more than seven miles distant offered a lovely little seclusion; and to this I had a privileged access; and at first I tried it, but it was a dressed and ornamented pleasure-ground: and two ladies of some distinction, nearly related to each other, and old friends of my mother, were in a manner the ladies paramount within the ring fence of this Arcadian vale. But this did not offer what I wanted. Everything was elegant, polished, quiet, throughout the lawns and groves of this verdant retreat: no rudeness was allowed here; even the little brooks were trained to 'behave themselves'.

Thomas de Quincey:
'Confessions of an English Opium-Eater' (1785-1859)

A Consideration
(On a February night,'86)

When the night flows suddenly
in February across these gardens,
spreading his gloom across the grove of trees
which sweeten the soil of the Dyke;
then, there comes to the air of my consciousness
the stirrings of my doubts,
to deceive me with their dark wings
from believing in the white Welshness
that has claimed, until now,
a little place in the sun
in the empire of my desire.

* * *

Where, in truth, in this place,
is the language concealed?

* * *

It is, I suppose, wrapped
in papers;
  documents,
    wills,
      intentions;
the withered roses of the past,
the red-brown petals of yesterday
that lie in the bottom drawers
of the odd valuable piece of oak furniture
in Rhosymedre, Acrefair, Cefnbychan,
Pentrebychan, Penycae and Rhos,
their petals tightly folded
against the rapaciousness that sparkles
in the greedy eyes of the grandchildren and great-grandchildren of the present.

She is also, certainly,
lying in beds,
in the damp scrapings of memories

of little old roses of women
in the old age homes of these parts.
the kind who moither about the pennies of their pensions
to the nervous nurses, in a strange language,
in Rhosymedre, Acrefair, Cefnbychan,
Pentrebychan, Penycae and Rhos.

That, perhaps, is where the language is hidden
in this place;
for what is said,
I fear,
on a narcotic February night
in Wrexham, to the Welsh language
is,
scram.

Bryan Martin Davies (1933 –)
Translated by Grahame Davies

Extremes of Topography

From rooftop level in Wrexham one's westward gaze roams over huddled villages and old colliery workings to the unobtrusive curve of purple moor above Minera. Eastward the foreground falls softly in wooded and pastured folds to the silent twisting Dee, beyond which nothing breaks the monotony till the sandstone hills of Bickerton and Peckforton like sleeping giants above the plain. The world thus embraced ranges between extremes of topography, geology, vegetation and human settlement. It is in fact two worlds – the world of the empty moors, the dark sentinels of the Welsh hills; and the world of the rich and wooded lowlands the English plain. Between the two lies Wrexham, a true border town.

But it is important to remember that the border has an infinitely longer history than the town. The border has always been a border, geographically, geologically, botanically and racially. Throughout prehistoric as well as historic times, its presence can be felt, its influence on settler and invader assessed. But in early times the site of the town was of no consequence. We look in vain here for the summer camps of Palaeolithic hunters, or the clearings of the first farmers; no Bronze Age necropolis or Iron Age *oppidum* sprang up on the banks of the Gwenfro. The local topography lacked these essentials which operate universally in the choice of primitive settlement. Here were no caves for shelter against the cold of the retreating ice – no fordable river, rich in fish; no open land, easy of tillage by digging-stick or foot-plough; no commanding hill for Iron Age camp or Roman fort. Hence a prehistory of Wrexham is a record of silence, a blank on the map.

W.E. Griffiths from 'A History of Wrexham' (1957)
Edited by A.H. Dodd

A Romantic Encounter

At Wrexham Church I glanced upon the face of a Miss E. Evans, a young lady with whom I have been in the habit of fraternal correspondence – She turned excessively pale – she thought it my Ghost, I suppose – I retreated with all possible speed to our Inn – there as I was standing at the window passed by Eliza Evans and with her, her sister, Mary Evans – quam efflictum et perdite amabam, (whom I loved madly and hopelessly) . . . I neither ate or slept yesterday – but Love is a local Anguish . . . I must endeavour to forget it amid the terrible Graces of the wildwood scenery that surrounds me . . .

Samuel Taylor Coleridge (1772-1834) in a letter to Robert Southey included in Joseph Hucks' 'A Pedestrian Tour Through North Wales'.

Snow in Wrexham

Yesterday,
  Snow was thick across the town,
acres of snow shivering
on the roofs and chimneys of the houses,
cataracts of snow freezing
on the walls and windows of the street,
floods of snow flowing
on glass and concrete and stone.
Yesterday,
  snow was thick across the town.

Like the familiar old language of the old high homeland,
it came to us for a trip to town,
Not as a thread of a consonant on the odd pleasant Saturday,
or a flake of a saying on market day,
it came,
  in a bright hoard of silver words,
  a dazzling ton of white syntax.

It came,
  and intricately conquered,
  for a day at least,
the broken patois of the town.

Yesterday,
  snow was thick across the town,
like a trembling of Welshness
from the tough mountain land,
like a flood of whiteness from Bwlchgwyn and Gwynfryn,
before today's thaw
estranges it to the crannies of the hills,
where it squats stubbornly
above the sad town.

Bryan Martin Davies (1933 –)
Translated by Grahame Davies

The Ladies of Llangollen

Eleanor Butler and Sarah Ponsomby have become known as 'the Ladies of Llangollen'. They were both born into Anglo-Irish aristocratic families, but eloped from Ireland in an attempt to escape their rigid, conventional backgrounds. The word 'eloped' is used deliberately here, for there can be little doubt, despite certain arguments to the contrary, that their relationship was sexual. They settled at Plas Newydd in Llangollen, a building which is now a popular tourist attraction. Following their arrival in 1780 the house became the focal point for many distinguished visitors, including the Duke of Wellington, Burke, Sir Walter Scott, Byron, Shelley and Wordsworth. Wordsworth composed a sonnet which offended the ladies; in it he described their home as 'a low-roofed cott'.

The ladies spent their days reading, gardening, playing backgammon and, according to one source, in 'dominating the life of Llangollen at the that time'. They also kept a journal, which despite its description of quite trivial events, does give us valuable insights into the lifestyle of two eccentric individuals.

'Tuesday, June 25th, 1791' – Walked down the green shady lane of Pengwern Hall. Saw the Bull in the next field. Retired in haste.
'Wednesday, June 26th' – A thought occurred relating to an improvement in the Dam and Pool next to the Mill. David the Miller accompanied us to the Quarry on the Mountain road to Llansanffraid Glynceiriog. Then got our Landlord's cart and team and with the assistance of David the Miller placed a range of flat stones in the Dam.
'Thursday, June 27th' – A little quizzical figure, and her maid with an umbrella paced up and down the field. A fine noble foreign looking copper coloured man with a thick black bushy beard, to all appearance is Turk or Greek, came for charity. Refused money. Accepted meat and drink. Spoke, but we could not understand what he said.
'Sunday, March 14th' – Went to our village church. An English sermon that might have been Hebrew for anything we understood of the matter, so deadly was it preached by the poor curate.
'Monday, March 15th' – At half-past ten in the Hand's new Chaise, Dick Morris driver – My Beloved and I went to Chirk Castle. Roads capital. A Porter at the gate. Drove up to the old entrance gate, alighted and walked through the great gates, found the Lawn covered with sheep and lambs, all milk-white. Found Mrs Middleton-Biddulph and Mrs Jones at Breakfast. Mrs M.B. received us with her usual kindness. Showed us the fine collection of Italian Books brought by

the late Col. Myddelton from Italy. Staid there a quarter of an hour and proceeded to Oswestry through the Park. Saw with regret the 64 old oak lying about which had been thrown down by the late tremendous storms. Met cattle innumerable driving from the fair. Stopped at little Edward the Bookseller's, paid him his bill. Left some newspapers to be bound. Next, to little Edward the Silversmith, bought a Pen knife, a silver pencil and gold locket, and some Honeysuckle Soap. We then went to Mrs Barrett's. Found her battling with a rebellious Tenant to whom she forgave thirty pounds arrears of rent. When the contest was over she and Margaret went with us round her ground.
'Wednesday, March 17th' – Fair in the village by much the poorest since we came to this Country, the season considered. Neither Beef nor Veal, the price of meat being so exorbitant that few can afford to purchase it. Many market days formerly were better attended, greater number of buyers and sellers than there are at this Fair.

Diary of Eleanor Butler (1739-1829) and Sarah Ponsomby (1755-1831)

Potations of Ale

On our arrival at the inn at Llangollen we found it in the possession of some mourners who had just returned from the funeral of a friend; however some tolerable quarters remained for us.

The dismal solemnity of these weeping countenances soon evaporated and the sorrows and senses of the company were quickly drowned in large potations of ale. Such is the general conclusion of a Welsh meeting, whether it be merry or melancholy.

Lord George Lyttleton
'A Gentleman's Tour Through Monmouthshire and Wales' (1774)

Out of Tune Trash

In 1829 the composer Felix Mendelssohn visited his friends the Taylor's at their home near Mold. He stayed for a week, during which he walked to Snowdonia.

Prior to his stay with the Taylor's he stayed at an inn at Llangollen and was in the process of writing home to a friend in Germany when he heard a harper playing some Welsh airs. His irrational anger is rather ironic, for nowadays the town is synonymous with international musical harmony.

Ten thousand devils take all national music! Here I am in Wales, and, heaven help us! a harper sits in the hall of every reputable tavern playing so called folk melodies – that is to say, dreadful, vulgar, out-of-tune, trash with a hurdy-gurdy going on at the same time!

It has given me toothache already. Scotch bagpipes. Swiss cow-horns, Welsh harps – all playing the Huntsman's Chorus with hideously improvised variations . . . It's unspeakable. Anyone who, like myself can't stand Beethoven's national songs ought to come to Wales and hear them bellowed by rough nasal voices to the crudest accompaniment – and then try to keep his temper. As I write a fellow in the hall is playing . . . it makes me so angry I can't go on.

Felix Mendelssohn (1809-1847)

In 1819 Michael Farraday, then a young man, toured North and South Wales and recorded his impressions in a journal.

The Pontycysyllty Aqueduct

We went down to the canal which is about mid way up from the bottom of the valley and keeping on its bank proceeded to the aqueduct. Where the canal first leaves this side of the mountain to cross the valley it proceeds for a great distance (1,500 feet) on an embankment raised by workmen and jutting out like a promontory. Then to continue the canal on the end of this embankment to the side of the valley opposite and across the River Dee many arches are raised upon slender stone here the highest of which is 120 ft. above the stream below. The number of arches is 18 and over the top of them the canal continues in a straight line with a path by the side of it for the horses and for foot passengers. This path is railed in on the outer edge and from every part of it presents beautiful views of the vale and River below and of the country around. After crossing the aqueduct we descended to the banks of the Dee and viewed the structure from below. It seemed light as a cloud.

Michael Farraday: 'Journal of a Tour Through Wales' (1819)

Llangollen Ale

While other poets loudly rant
About Llangollen's Vale,
Let me, with better taste, descant
Upon Llangollen Ale.

The daughters of the place are fair,
Its sons are strong and hale:
What makes them so? Llangollen air?
No, no! – Llangollen Ale.

And Nature only beautified
The landscape, to prevail
On travellers to turn aside
And quaff Llangollen Ale.

For though the scene might please at first
Its charms would quickly stale;
While he who tastes will ever thirst
To drink Llangollen Ale.

In short, each ruin, stream, or tree,
Within Llangollen's Tale,
Wherever I turn, whate'er I see,
Is redolent of Ale.

Anon (19th century)

A Bloody Conflict

From hence I hastened towards *Chirk* castle, keeping a lower road between the two dikes. On approaching the village of *Chirk*, is a very deep valley, consisting of fertile meadows, watered by the brook *Ceiriog*, and finely bounded by lofty wooded banks. On the very verge of that next to *Chirk*, stands an artificial mount; and, I think, the vestige of another, on the other side of the road which goes between them. These were exploratory, and probably designed also for defence; and might have had on them a small fort for the protection of the pass. I imagine these mounts to have been *Saxon*, and coeval with the great labor of *Offa*, which runs at a small distance from them.

In this deep valley which winds along the foot of the vast *Berwyn* mountains, was a bloody conflict between part of the forces of *Henry* II and the *Welsh*, in 1165. *Henry* had determined once more to attempt the subjection of *Wales*, and to revenge the ravages carried through the borders by its gallant prince *Owen Gwynedd*; for that end, he assembled a vast army at *Oswestry*. *Owen*, on the contrary, collected all his chieftains, with their dependants, at *Corwen*. The king, hearing that his antagonist was so near, resolved to bring the matter to a speedy decision. He marched towards him; and in this valley, finding himself entangled in impenetrable woods, and recollecting his ill-fortune among the forests of *Eulo*, directed his vanguard to make the passage clear by cutting down the trees, in order to secure himself from ambuscade. The pikemen, and flower of his army, were posted to cover the workmen. The spirit of the common soldiers of the *Welsh* army grew indignant at this attempt; and, without the knowledge of their officers, fell with unspeakable fury on these troops. The contest was violent; numbers of brave men perished; in the end, the *Welsh* retired to *Corwen*. *Henry* gained the summit of the *Berwyn*; but was so distressed by dreadful rains, and by the activity and prudence of *Owen*, who cut him off from all supplies, that he was obliged to return ingloriously, with great loss of men and equipage.

This conflict is sometimes called the battle of *Corwen*; but with more propriety that of *Crogen*; for it happened beneath *Castelh Crogen*, the present *Chirk* castle; and the place still called *Adwy'r Beddau*, or the *pass of the graves* of the men who were slain here.

Thomas Pennant (1726-1798) From 'Tours in Wales'

Stirring History

The history of border districts is proverbially a stirring one. Whether handed down in all the glories of *The Ballad of Chevy Chase*, or in the brief phrases of an old chronicle, it carries with it those elements of romance inseparable from the clash of two races, and the struggle for a 'debatable land'. Chirkland is no exception to this rule. For so small and thinly populated a district its fortunes have often been, to a surprising degree, in the main stream of national history.

This is mainly attributable to two causes: first, its situation, and second, its possession, at different periods, by certain persons of marked personality. The unconquerable independence of the Welsh people, leading to continual resistance to English rule, gave the line of border castles between the two countries a peculiar importance. Chirk

Castle, as commanding two routes between England and Wales – those of the Dee and Ceiriog valleys – must often have been one of the keys of the situation.

Margaret Mahler: 'The History of Chirk Castle and Chirkland' (1912)

A God-Fearing People

Philip Henry's diary is recognised as a document of major interest for any student of seventeenth century history in North Wales.

Henry began life as an Anglican and became a minister at a time when persecution on religious grounds was common place.

He was a highly educated man and was appointed as tutor to the sons of Judge John Puleston at Emral in English Maelor.

In his border country ministry his days as a propagator of Puritan theology were cut short by the Restoration of 1660, and he was forced to leave Worthenbury. Many ploys had been made to discredit him, including the enforcement of minor legal loopholes.

His diary remained unpublished until 1882. Here are some extracts:

I felled two ashes and an oak for implements for husbandry. In falling one of the ashes, it pleased God wonderfully to preserve Daniel Powel, the son of Margaret Powel, aged 8 years. The tree fell upon him but he escaped the body and fell under the outermost boughs, so that he received no harm. Blessed be the name of the Lord.

Ann Hale deprehended in two or three thefts, a cup, a dish, scollop work, all trifling matters, yet see the power of temptation.

About this time a great appearance of fire was seen in this neighbourhood and elsewhere. What it portends God knows. One about Shrewsbury, they say, fortells three battles this year, one whereof upon Prees Heath, and I am asked what I think of it. I answered I cannot let the event speak.

An exceeding bitter cold season, the frost continuing with small intermissions these many weeks.

At Chester I heard of the imprisonment of Mr Yates, Minister of Harrington, upon the malicious information of a person of small credit, who swore he moved him to take up arms against the King for the Presbyterians and promised him 40 pence a week pay.

Went to see Mr Adams of Iscoyd Hall, whose house had been robbed this last week, bacon and beef being taken away. Morning prayer with my wife omitted for some weeks, this day revived – Lord never let me alone in sin.

John Beard of Whitchurch buried two children of the smallpox in the compass of one week; Lord what mercy it is that mine are spared.

Hawthorn – sets planted to hedge in the orchard. Lord be thou a wall of fire round about thy Church and let not the wild boar of the forest devour your tender plants. Fodder scarce and dear; we did ill not to provide in Summer for Winter.

I went to Wrexham with intentions to sell my mare at the fair, but could not. It grieves me very much to see how the Presbyterian interest there, which I judge the middle of two extremes, is of late eclipsed and clouded, the cause I judge to be want of communion amongst them, and the cause of that want of a faithful minister to go before them.

I went to see Margaret Bedward, sick and tempted. I judge it a melancholy humour prevailing, which the devil works upon the disturbing of her peace. She thought the Devil persuaded her to give hers to him. I prayed with her – Lord hear prayer. I met two or three friends at Cousin Benet's to seek God on behalf of our poor tempted friend. Lord command Satan to depart from her, and bring good out of it.

Headache, indigestion and other bodily distempers, fruits of sin, fore-runners of dissolution. I thought once this day, I could not only be willing but rejoice to die, that I might be with the Lord.

A youth of 17 or 18 years of age riding between Shrewsbury and Wrexham, there hanging a bough of a tree over the way. He pushed it back with his hand and it fluttered in his face and struck him into his eye and brain whereby this day he died in Wrexham.

William Lack told me of a woman in Hope parish who hearing those words pronounced that whereby scandalous livers are warned not to come to the holy table, she was struck in conscience and fell into great terrors. The Minister, Mr Jones, being sent for told her he did not mean her to take his sermon to her private heart, gave her an amulet of some verses from John I written on a piece of paper to hang around her neck, as also certain herbs to drive the devil out of her, but all in vain. Her brother and William Lack being sent for, they gave her counsel and prayed with her several times till at length she was much better and they hope good work is wrought on her, her husband saying he is sure she is a better wife since than she ever was before.

Philip Henry (1631-1696) from his Diary

Welsh Frankton

Tom Strange, my grandfather, came to Welsh Frankton, just a few miles from Ellesmere, in the late 1800's to work as a smith for the nearby Hardwick Hall, but taking on work on his own account too.

I know little about him except that he is said to have been much in the mould of the traditional smith, being big, broad and strong.

I remember an old photograph of him that hung oppressively in one of the bedrooms in our house. He reminded me then, with his long black beard and wide brimmed black hat, of one of those evil figures who used to stalk the old silent movies.

Dad told us of how grandad used to test the strength of job applicants by hurling a sixteen pound hammer through the smithy door and asking the prospective employee to match the throw. Few managed to do it, but old Tom Strange had the tables turned on him on one occasion when the new man, seeing no suitable hammer about, picked up the much heavier anvil and not only matched, but bettered the effort. He must have wanted the job badly.

Were Tom Strange able to return to Welsh Frankton today he would see changes that have taken place gradually, but which have changed dramatically both the face and the heart of the village and its surrounding hamlets during the past eighty years.

Welsh Frankton itself sits astride Frankton Brow – a sudden rise in the land that lies between the Shropshire market towns of Oswestry and Ellesmere.

From the top of the Brow on a clear day you can see almost to Chester on the Dee to the north; while far to the south the great Wrekin is in plain view. To the west the snow capped hills of Wales sweep down to the border flatlands around Oswestry, and to the east the chimneys of Ellesmere can be seen above the trees.

Tetchill lies hidden about two miles distant, off the road to Ellesmere, but spires of smoke mark the line of Lower Frankton as it ribbons its way down the Brow towards the Llangollen Canal. Closer still are the hamlets of Higher Ridge, Lower Ridge and the Perthy, where I was born. They lie peacefully, all part of the same straggling community, amidst the Shropshire greenery that holds the eye wherever you look.

The beauty of the place has held me throughout my life. I have moved house only once, from my old smithy on the Perthy to my farm-cum-smithy here on the Brow, a distance of about fifty yards.

The general layout of the village has changed little since the beginning of the century but grandad would have noticed things like the disappearance of the Perthy smithy where he spent much of his life.

The dirt road that once ran over the Brow and down past the Green Man pub has long gone too. The old horse track is now a fast tarmac-adamed through route to Whitchurch, and the pub has long since been a farmhouse.

In fact none of the old pubs that he would remember in the village have survived and even the 'high' school (so named because of its position on the Brow, rather than the level of its education) has closed and now operates as a trailer works.

New people, a new type of people are starting to occupy the village now. The old style villagers who lived and worked in the community are fast disappearing; driven out by modern economics, attracted to the advantages of town living, or just dying off.

Alf Strange: My Dad's the Village Blacksmith' (1983)

The Kingdom of Sphagnum

'No words that I know of will say what mosses are'

John Ruskin

Whixall Moss and Fenn's Moss, 2000 acres between Shropshire and Clwyd

The Boundary

Bark border
of the peat prairie: forest
where birds have freehold,
lichen has license.
Fox-haven; weasel covert;
home of vole and smaller than vole.

Barbed wire slices saplings –
teeth biting into bark
are absorbed, become part
of the growing tree.
Logs piled in pyramids,
like threshold guardians,
warn of selective felling.

Maps show other borders:
radial band of road,
the canal's slow coil,
a railway's relentless parallels.
Fixed lines on the map
demarcations of territory –
here is Wales, there England,
this segment Shropshire, that corner Clwyd.
False frontiers invaded by winds,
by seeds, spores, germs.
On the winds the whisper of languages
blown either way, reversing directions.
No line fractures the bog –
Whixall, Fenn's, Oaf's Orchard,
the given names for one being –
no margins in the mosses
the kingdom of sphagnum
where space and time are interwoven.

The blue line on the map
depicts water – a solid straightness
of canal; there a wiggle of river,
a filament of stream.
Yet all here is liquid,
names labelling a wilderness of water,
water disguised, gone under,
hiding beneath the levels.
Peat-cloaked, this water's
palomino, pewter.

Fifteen miles of road, a tarmac torc.
Buildings are few, crouch at the fringe
with the air of trespassers:
self-conscious, sagging shacks,
red-brick rows of peat-workers,
untidy farms encroaching
like lice on the shaggy coat
of a great beast.
The bog breathes, renews, moves,
is their warden, their time-keeper
impressing upon them their impermanence.

Snowdrops. A house was here,
half-way habitat at the wood's edge,
poised between wilderness and wild.
The white surprise among dereliction –
uncountable clusters, minute nuns
praying in a weed garden. Witnesses
to births and deaths, the rise and fall
of structures. Moss has crept
where quoins once were; lichen claims
a crumbling fence; hart's tongue fern
flames in the hearth-place.

Another house gone blind, abandoned.
One Sixties car and a lorry left,
rusty as red sphagnum. Their grills grin,
deathmasks of chrome; dormice's den.
Gorse gains ground under their chassis,
moss embeds their wheels. Rooted,
these vehicles warn the Star-Trek people –
sad fairground wintering here –
be itinerant, travel on.

I come alone, savouring solititude,
seeking to slice through time,
feel inner frost melt,
rediscover my own space.
The past is an eye-blink away;
the peat is an archive,
an age of ice underground;
the grain close-packed,
a tangible reservoir.

Give Way. The notice blares at a crossroads.
Go back The caution ricochets through dead heather.
I advance onto the open plain. – *No further, no further!*
This is not your place!

Gladys Mary Coles (1994)

A False Alarm

Askew Roberts was a native of Oswestry, where he spent most of his life. He was involved with the world of local journalism and founded the 'Oswestry Advertiser'. It was his idea to include the antiquarian column 'Bye Gones' in that paper, and historians still turn to the column today in their search for out of the way historical gems. His diary is unpublished and the two brief extracts below appear in print for the first time.

1st January, 1868: The year has opened with alarms, some serious and others absurd. The disordered state of Ireland and the daring acts of Americanised Irishmen at Clerkenwell and Manchester has quite set the nation by the ears.

An epidemic broke out in Oswestry and was caused by some joker, who sent a letter through the Oswestry Post Office addressed 'Col.Mulready, RIFB (Royal Irish Fenian Brotherhood), Liverpool, to be called for'. Of course, this wasn't called for, as it was sent to the Home Office, and forwarded to George Saunders, our mayor, with a somewhat sharp reproof.

On the 1st February and earlier during the night of 31st January, there was a fearful storm of wind and rain in Montgomeryshire. The embankment of the bridge over the Severn gave way and an engine was precipitated into the floods, the driver and fireman being killed. The bridge at Pontdolgoch was also considerably damaged. Near to Llanfyllin a post boy was driving home an empty carriage and was drowned in what is normally a fordable rivulet crossing the road, and near Llansanffraid two men were drowned in a field, so suddenly did the water rise.

From the diary of Askew Roberts (1826-1884)
Deposited in the Denbighshire Record Office Ref. DD/GL/143

Tim Liardet is a widely published poet and critic who lives in Oswestry. This poem was specially commissioned for this anthology.

Baloonists over Oswestry

The church-tower broadening earthwards quits
Ascending as inflated silks continue to rise.
The tower tilts away, at sea. The slow balloon
Bit by bit, is taking its grasp of consciousness:
From such a height every pane must flash,
The nucleus draw in its flung fragments.
The centre itself must seem to turn slowly,
must seem to swirl, a little froth trapped
By opposing currents, nurtured on chaos, listing with the town:

The other way's harder. The physical climb
Inside the tower where steps and a stained rope guiding
A few through dull bulbs up to greater light
Is slow and arduous. All who cleave to the rope
Must make their pausing way up into the wind
For a view of their town, at length, to pick
From sixty feet their distant homes and be able
To hear beneath trembling silks gas-turbines roar
Overhead, passing slowly, eerie in daylight.

Many make the long climb, but not that often:
They will note, like balloonists, how the awning
Dips across the street but hardly moves at all
How the fête's stalls shine – in brilliance–
How the lit hotel, bank, antiquarian bookshop,
The Coach and Dogs and traffic-lights could not
Be anywhere else, how the defunct track
Halts at its boarded station and the young mens' cars
Complete another circuit of the one-way system.

But drifting North, away from the unheavenly promise
Of Birmingham in its fog of turbulence,
Towards the air of open valley, rock and water –
The Ceiriog twisting in and out of England and Wales –
The slow balloonists drift higher. From there,

The school grounds and lit mustard beyond
Are flown by cloud-shadows that roll up
The cricket team like a rug of jewels;
The Dee loops, a deciduous darkness hugs –

A path through the high grass is flattened
By the passage of a single walker;
The long shining roads converge upon *The Cross*
Around which a settlement of roof-ridges
And rabble of birds and chimneys seems to cling,
Anchoring the roads by which it is reached,
By which it is left. Balloonists breathe mountain air –
At three times the church-tower's height the turbines
Putter out, after flame, glide in silence –

Silence. Fathoms of it. Death's visage. Camera lucida.
The whole town tilts up and swings round. The charred gape
Of the dead industrial chimney leans away.
Brought back perpetually to the point at which
They all began, passing the boarded warehouses
And the grassed-over hill fort the young men's cars
Like old assumptions, generations, like local knowledge
Endlessly circuit the one-way system,
Their tiny rooves effulgent, their revs inaudible.

Tim Liardet (1996)

The Kyffins and the Trevors

It was the manner in those days that the murderer only and he that gave the death wound should only fly, which was called in Welsh a *llawrudd*, which is a 'red hand' because he had blooded his hand. The accessories and abettors to the murder, they were never hearkened after.

In those days in Chirkland and in Oswestryland two sects or kindreds contended for the sovereignty of the country and were at continual strife one with another, the Kyffins and Trefors. They had their alliance, partisans and friends in all countries round thereabouts to whom, as the manner of that time was, they sent such of their followers as committed murder or manslaughter, who were safely kept as very precious jewels, and they received the like from their friends. This kind of people were stowed in the daytime in chambers in their houses and in the night they went to the next winehouse that belonged to the gentleman or to his tenants' houses not far off to make merry and to wench.

Maredudd ap Hywel ap Morus, in those days chief and leader of the sect of the Kyffins, was a kin to Ieuan ap Robert and in league with him; to whom he sent to desire him to draw him a draft to catch those murderers. [He] sent him word that he should come privately into Chirkland only accompanied but with six, and he made no doubt to deliver the murderers into his hands.

As Ieuan ap Robert was on his way going thither passing by Tŷ-yn-Rhos (being a winehouse standing in Penrhyndeudraeth), Hywel ap Rhys ap Hywel Fychan's wife, being in the house, said to the people that were with her: 'Yonder goes Ieuan ap Robert: *Hwyr y dial fo i dadmaeth*', which is as much [as] to say that he would not in haste be revenged of the wrong done to his foster.

Being come to Chirkland he abode there many days in secret and, unseen, sleeping in the day and watching all night. In the end, with the help of his friends, he caught the two murderers which he had no sooner in hand but the cry arose. The Trefors to their friends and the Kyffins to their leader, Maredudd ap Hywel ap Morus, resorted, who told Ieuan ap Robert that it was impossible for him to carry them out of the country to any place to have judicial proceeding against them by reason of the faction of the Trefors [which] would lay the way and narrow passages of the country, and if they were brought to Chirk castle gate to receive the trial of that country's laws it was lawful for the offenders' friends (whosoever they were) to bring five pounds for every man for a fine to the lord and to acquit them, so it were not in cases of treason. A damnable custom used in those days in the lordships marchers which was used also in Mawddwy until the new ordinance of Wales made in [the] twenty seventh [year] of Henry the Eighth. Hereupon, Ieuan ap Robert ap Maredudd commanded one of his men to strike off their heads which, the fellow doing faintly, the offender told him that if he had his [i.e. the executioner's] neck under his sword he would make his sword take better edge than he did, so resolute were they in those days and in contempt of death. Whereupon Ieuan [ap] Robert, in a rage, stepping to them struck off their heads.

Sir John Wynn (1553-1627): 'History of the Gwydir Family' (c.1570)

Iolo Goch was a native of the Vale of Clwyd. Like many of the poets of his period he was dependent on the patronage of the gentry. The culture of the period held poets to be socially important and they were systematically trained before being accepted for admission to the bardic order. Iolo, who is thought by many to be buried at Valle Crucis Abbey, was much favoured by Owain Glyndŵr in his latter years and while a member of the court of the great leader at Sycharth wrote the following poem of praise.

Sycharth

'Tis water girdled wide about
It shows a wide and stately door
Reached by a bridge the water o'er
'Tis formed of buildings coupled fair,
Coupled is every couple there;
Within a quadrate structure tall,
Master the merry pleasures all.
Co-jointly are the angles bound –
No flaw in all the place is found.
Structures in contact meet the eye
Upon the hillocks top on high;
Into each other fastened they
The form of a hard knot display.
There dwells the chief we all extoll
In timber house on lightsome knoll
Upon four wooden columns proud
Each column thick and firmly bas'd
And upon each a loft is placed;
In these four lofts which coupled stand
Repose at night the minstrel band;
Four lofts they were in pristine state
But now, partitioned, form they eight.
Tiled is the roof, on each house top
Rise smoke-ejecting chimneys up
All of one form there are nine halls
Each with nine wardrobes within its walls
With linen white as well supplied
As fairest shops in famed Cheapside
Behold that church with cross upraised
And with its windows neatly glazed.

All houses are in this compress –
An orchard's near it of the best.
Also a park where void of fear
Feed antlered herds of fallow deer.
A warren wide my chief can boast.
Of goodly steeds a countless host.
Meads where for hay the clover grows,
Cornfields which hedges trim enclose
A mill a rushing brook upon,
And pigeon tower fram'd of stone.
A fishpond deep and dark to see
To cast nets in when need there be
Which never yet was known to lack
A plenteous store of perch and jack
Of various plumage birds abound
Herons and peacocks haunt around
What luxury doth his hall adorn
Showing of cost a sovereign scorn
His ale from Shrewsbury town he brings.
His usquebagh is drink for kings;
Bragget he keeps, bread white of look
And, bless the mark, a bustling cook
His mansion is the minstrel's home
You'll find them there when'er you come
Of all her sex his wife's the best;
The household through her care is blest;
She's scion of a knightly tree,
She's dignified, she's kind and free
His bairns approach me, pair by pair,
Oh what a nestful of chieftains there
Here difficult it is to catch
A sight of either bolt or latch
The porters place here none will fill;
Here largesse shall be lavished still
And ne'er shall thirst or hunger rude
In Sycharth venture to intrude.
A noble leader, Cambria's knight,
The lake possesses, his by right
And in that azure water placed
The castle by each pleasure grac'd.

Iolo Goch (c.1320-1398)
Translated by George Borrow

An Enduring Heritage

It was not from a borough or a garrison town but from one of the glens of the Dee that Owain Glyndŵr rose to wage his fifteen years' memorable struggle for Wales. Huw Morris, Pont y Meibion, and Morgan Llwyd o Wynedd, the two Welsh voices of the seventeenth century, were country folk. So were all the leaders of the religious revival. Thomas Charles and Lewis Edwards came from peasant hearths. Diosg Farm sheltered the three famous brothers of Llanbrynmair, pioneers of Welsh reform. William Rees and Henry Rees, who from this city wielded so strong and noble an influence over their countrymen, were nurtured at Chwibren Isa, in the free bracing air of the Hiraethog hills. From cottages nestling under the Berwyns have sprung typical men like Ceiriog, Ieuan Gwynedd, and Owen Edwards. And there is no reason to suppose that the country districts will cease to form the nursery ground of men of thought, initiative, and influence.

T.E. Ellis (1859-1899)
from 'Speeches and Addresses' (1912)

The Arrival of Coleridge

The great English essayist and critic William Hazlitt was born in Kent, but spent much of his youth at Wem. Here he describes a turning point in his intellectual development.

My father was a Dissenting minister at Wem, in Shropshire, and in the year 1798 Mr Coleridge came to Shrewsbury to succeed Mr Rowe in the spiritual charge of a Unitarian congregation there. He did not come till late on the Saturday afternoon before he was to preach, and Mr Rowe, who himself went down to the coach in a state of anxiety and expectation to look for the arrival of his successor, could find no one at all answering the description but a round-faced man in a short black coat (like a shooting-jacket) which hardly seemed to have been made for him, but who seemed to be talking at a great rate to his fellow-passengers. Mr Rowe had scarce returned to give an account of his disappointment when the round-faced man in black entered, and dissipated all doubts on the subject by beginning to talk. He did not cease while he stayed, nor has he since, that I know of. He held the good town of Shrewsbury in delightful suspense for three weeks that he remained there, 'fluttering the *proud Salopians* like an eagle in a dove-cote;' and the Welsh mountains that skirt the horizon with their tempestuous confusion agree to have heard no such mystic sounds since the days of

'High-born Hoel's harp or soft Llewellyn's lay'.

As we passed along between Wem and Shrewsbury, and I eyed their blue tops seen through the wintry branches, or the red rustling leaves of the sturdy oak-trees by the road-side, a sound was in my ears as of a Syren's song; I was stunned, startled with it, as from deep sleep; but I had no notion then that I should ever be able to express my admiration to others in motley imagery or quaint allusion, till the light of his genius shone into my soul, like the sun's rays glittering in the puddles of the road . . ..

My father lived ten miles from Shrewsbury, and was in the habit of exchanging visits with Mr Rowe, and with Mr Jenkins, of Whitchurch (nine miles further on), according to the custom of Dissenting ministers in each other's neighbourhood. A line of communication is thus established, by which the flame of civil and religious liberty is kept alive, and nourishes its smouldering fire unquenchable, like the fires in the *Agamennon* of Eschylus, placed at different stations, that waited for ten long years to announce with their blazing pyramids the destruction of Troy. Coleridge had agreed to come over and see my father, according to the courtesy of the country, as Mr Rowe's probable successor; but, in the meantime, I had gone to hear him preach the Sunday after his arrival. A poet and a philosopher getting up into a Unitarian pulpit to preach the Gospel was a romance in these degenerate days, a sort of revival of the primitive spirit of Christianity which was not to be resisted.

William Hazlitt (1778-1830) from 'My First Acquaintance with Poets'

Black Barren

Aye, lad, I sold the last batch of lambs at the mart yesterday. A fair enough price they fetched too. Mind you, the ewes are yearning: been bleating away all night long. I didn't wean the lambs this year: only sold them off as they came ready. It's all early lambs now. Aye, the poor old ewes are yearning. Like to see them? I'm just going to have a look at them now.

Sheep are my life, you know. Fond of sheep I am. If I was a poet

I'd write an ode about sheep. The lambs are so pretty in the spring, bouncing like snowflakes all over the meadow; I can watch them for hours. A pity they have to grow. Still, there's something attractive about them at every age – like people, I suppose. Take yearlings now; smart they are; in the bloom of life, as you might say. A penful of warm wethers, out of breath after gathering; there's nothing like pushing through them, feeling them, enjoying them with the tips of my fingers. Kind old mother ewes like these I'm going to show you now. A proper Samson of a ram, head up, staring into the distance, pleased with himself after a good season's work. And the odd old barren that couldn't take a ram, empty in a field full of in-lambs. Feel sorry for them I do. Nature's hard on some.

Aye, I've got a barren or two every year. But I've got one – if she's really mine – you'll see her in a moment – I've had her for twenty years. Hard to believe, isn't it? Black she is, with two curly horns like a Welsh ram. Curlier if anything. Where she came from I haven't a clue. Perhaps you can explain it when you see her. But I'm telling you: she's been here twenty years, and growing bigger every day. She's bigger than any ram I've ever had. She's huge. But you'll see for yourself in a moment.

I'll tell you when I saw her first. I'd just been to Oswestry mart buying two dozen ewes. I'd turned them into the field and had my tea. After milking and letting the cows out, I popped over to see how the ewes were settling down. And damn, there she was, black and horny among them. An ugly, skinny, long-legged thing, staring at me like any cheeky brat.

Well, the following Wednesday I went to the mart. I'd bought the ewes off a chap from down-country, round Clun that way, a redhead, name of Briggs. I went up to him and told him that I'd bought two dozen ewes off him but that I didn't want the ugly black one that he'd put in with them, and would he take her back? God, no, he hadn't sold me a black ewe. She was never his. He hadn't had a black sheep on his land.

I was in a bit of a fog now, like. I went round the neighbours. No, none of them had lost a black sheep. I went to the policeman. I told the sheep-steward. And I put a small add in the local paper. Then I waited. Heard nothing. No one claimed her. And of course she had no ear markings as she's obviously never been on a mountain and no red paint or any mark of any kind on her wool.

Well, I said to myself, I've got a black sheep. Nobody owns her. Or, at any rate, nobody claims to. It's as if she's dropped from another world. I'm telling you, I'd hated her at first sight, but I could do nothing now but keep her.

Right. The hard winter came. That winter, if you remember, when it rained ice. Inches of ice on top of feet of snow, every twig and blade of grass cased in a finger of ice. All these Berwyn mountains were like glass. I was having to carry dry hay to the flock; I carried, and kept on carrying, load after load. They'd stuck in a row at the top of the slope behind the house, and I had to strap each burden of hay on my back and crawl up towards them on all fours. And when I'd almost reached the top I'd slither back down the slope to the bottom and had to start all over again. The hay had finished in the loft above the shippon and I was watching the hay in the dutch barn falling lower and lower every day, with no sign of an end to the freeze-up. I was tiring, and I was worrying.

The sheep had gone almost too weak to eat. But this black sheep, she ate like a hungry horse. She'd munch heartily under the others' noses. She'd snatch hay from their mouths. I never saw anything like it. And then, the fever started. The ewes were dying one by one, and not from cold. The ewes that died were those with twin lambs inside them. I carried one after the other into the shippon and laid them in the alley in front of the cattle's steaming nostrils to give them some warmth. The alley was full of them, like a row of woolly skeletons, but die they did, do what I might to save them. But do you think there was any chance of that old black barren dying? No fear, lad. While the others died in heaps in the alley, she stood at the top of the slope in the teeth of every blizzard, *growing*. I'd never seen her look better than she did that winter. She hadn't got twin lambs inside her like those that were dying. She'd got nothing inside her except hunger.

The winter passed, but I'd come to hate this old black sheep so much that I decided to sell her. When mid-spring came I picked five other barrens and put her with them, and off I went to the mart. I got precious little for them, but I was quite glad to be rid of them; pasture was scant enough. Fine, I said: that one's gone, and good riddance to her.

But hell, when I got home and went to look at the ewes that were still dropping lambs, what should I see right among them, as bold as ever, but her. Great heaven, I said, how did *she* come all the way back here, when I've just sold her ten miles away? She was like a big black blot among my little white sheep, staring at me like a curse.

That, for a while, was that. The time came to wash the sheep ready for shearing. And I washed her, though I'd meant not to. I hated the thought of putting her murky black fleece with the white wool of the others. Anyway, I was standing at the edge of the washing-pool with a wooden douser in my hand, ducking each sheep with it on the neck as she passed, holding her under water for a minute or so. Then Dick, Gelli, threw in the black barren, though he swore afterwards that he didn't. Well, first of all, she made such a splash that I was wet from head to foot. Then the douser got caught in her fleece, as if that cursed wool of hers had curled itself round it. The next thing I knew was that I was with her up to my neck in the mucky water. To finish the job properly she landed me a crunching kick in the ribs before leaping over the floodgate after the others. Taking revenge on me she was. You can laugh, lad, but I know that's what it was.

That year passed, and the year after. The black barren wasn't behaving too badly now, but I hated the sight of her. If she'd produce a lamb to pay for her keep that would be something, but she was good for nothing as she was. All she did was grow. She stood head and shoulders above every other sheep on the place, her horns like two coiled snakes on either side of her head.

I'd just bought a new ram. A big Leicester. A noble creature with a nose like an eagle's beak and white socks and a fine carpet of wool on him. He'd served all the ewes in his field as far as I could judge, except the black barren. Oh, I said to myself, she won't take this one either. The murky madam was keeping a field's breadth away from him.

But one evening, what should I see but her and the big Leicester together in the corner of the field. So, I said, she'd found her lord and master after all. I might get a lamb from her this time, though I hope it'll be a better thing than she is. And I went home feeling oddly satisfied. Next morning I returned to the field. The big Leicester was lying dead as a doornail, his belly torn open by a pair of horns.

I went home at once, crying like a child. That ram had cost money. I snatched the gun from its corner, loaded it and ran back to the field. She was grazing on her own on the hillock, grazing fast and furious as if she were starving. You *shall* starve, my beauty, I said – for ever. I'd never had a better target. It was as if she'd been set there for me.

I raised the gun. I aimed. I fired. But just as I fired, she moved. And what should I see behind her but another ewe that had been grazing in her shadow. That one dropped dead, her head full of shot. But the black barren? None the worse. She carried on grazing fast and furious; the shot hadn't even disturbed her.

I nearly shot myself. That was the next thought that came to me. I couldn't fire again on the black barren lest I killed another of my precious ewes. It was the first time she really put fear into me. I was sick with fear.

But the following day would be Wednesday. You wait till tomorrow morning, my lovely, I said, and you'll go. This time for sure. But when the next day came she didn't go. Whether it was the fear or not I can't say, but I felt too weak to go to the mart. So she stayed.

She kept on growing. Year after year she grew. She's grown twice as big as the rams. I sheared her, but her fleece was useless. It was frittered away in my hands. And she never bore a lamb. A barren she was, by nature.

Anyway, one evening I was rounding up the sheep. It was hot, sultry weather with thunder about, and a lot of the sheep were crawling with maggots. It fairly hurt me to see them, twisting and turning and raking themselves against the posts in the hedges, their backs raw naked flesh. But her? Oh, she was fine, grazing away in mid-field, her useless fleece whole and her skin as healthy as could be, without a fly or a maggot near her. God, I got mad. I was that tired after being at it for hours on end with the shears and the ointment, and here was this evil creature as fit as a fiddle amid all the suffering. I just couldn't stand it. I crept quietly up behind her, caught her round the throat with my crook and held her. She was strong and kicked like a horse, but I held on. I managed to pull some cord from my rucksack, fettered her feet, and threw her on the grass. Then I took out my clasp-knife.

Now, Lady Soot, I said, we'll see which of us is the stronger. It's not a gun I've got this time: there's no danger of my killing one of the others. I'm going to finish you. My life's not worth living.

I grasped her throat, spreading the wool to make a clear space for the blade, then raised my hand high enough for one clean blow. But just as the knife was on its way down she looked at me, her eyes afire, and gave a sharp shudder. And the blade plunged into my left wrist. The last thing I saw was my own blood. After that, all went black.

When I came round, I was lying in the house with the doctor bending over me. Dick, Gelli, had happened to come by and had seen me flat on the field, bleeding. I asked him what about the black sheep. He'd seen no black sheep, only a piece of tangled cord on the grass at my elbow.

I must have lost pints of blood. I lay for three days, and it was some time before I got strong enough to take a walk round the fields.

But when I did, the first thing I looked for was her. If I hadn't seen her I would have felt strangely disappointed. But she was there, right enough. She was all there.

Till then, I'd been fighting her, and I didn't know for sure which of us was master. But the fighting came to an end. And this is how it happened.

There's an outcrop of rock about a quarter of a mile from here. Evans' Rock we call it, because there was a quarry of some sort there many years ago. On this side the land is level, but on the other there's a sheer drop of several hundred feet. I'd had to put up a strong fence round it to prevent the sheep and heifers and young steers from getting near it, because I'd lost more than one lamb that had fallen over, and I'd found a heifer on it once with a broken leg. Not one of the sheep had got through that fence. But milady got through it, as you might expect. She'd get through anything.

If she'd gone on her own I could have forgiven her. But she drew three yearling ewes with her. And when I saw them they were standing in a huddle on the highest boulder. My heart took a turn when I saw them. How the devil am I going to get those from there without frightening them over the edge? I said to myself. Somehow, I'll have to catch them and fetter them and carry them one by one on my back.

Well, I tied the dog to the corner post in the fence and started to crawl towards them on all fours, moving as stealthily as I could from boulder to boulder, keeping my head well down. I was close by them now, and they hadn't see me. But I had to come into sight because there was a strip of open ground between us. My heart pounded like a mallet as I thought of that precipice beneath them: one slip would be enough.

Very slowly I raised my head. And she saw me. It was she, the black barren, that saw me first, you can be sure. She bleated and stamped her foot. One of the yearlings took fright, and jumped, and fell into the gulley below. Well, that's the end of that one, I said. A pretty young ewe that would have bred for years.

On I went, gnashing my teeth. When I was within five yards the black barren spun like a top and pushed one of the remaining yearlings with her rump, sending her spinning into the abyss with a long-drawn-out cry like a child's.

I was crying myself now. I couldn't help it. There was only one thing I could do: rescue the last little yearling, come what might. So I reached out my crook as gently as I could, trying to get the handle round her throat before she could jump. But just before the crook reached her what should the old black barren do but plant her horns under the yearling and lift her. And the last one vanished out of my sight in that awful depth.

I stood up then and cursed the barren, I don't need to tell you. I cursed her to hell and beyond, 'You go after them!' I shouted, my tears spurting. 'Go, damn you! Go!' She just stood there, her black lips curled off her teeth in a maddening leer. And if I was ever maddened I was maddened then. I gripped my crook and gave her a ferocious prod with the ferrule, and another, and another. But I couldn't move her. It was like as if her hooves had been soldered to the rock. And d'you know what she did next? Her leer died on her lips, and she gave me a most pitiful look as if she were saying, 'Are you going to leave me on this old rock to starve?'

I suddenly felt strange all over. I just couldn't stare her in the eye. And the next thing I knew was that I'd lifted her, huge as she was, on my shoulders and was lurching with her over the rocks and slippery grass back towards the fence. I set her down in the field. She turned once and looked at me like the devil himself, as much as to say, 'You silly fool'. And off she went.

I knew that the fighting was over. There was little doubt now who was master.

Well, there we are. I'll just open this gate and we'll go into the field. There they are, see, the old ewes. Still bleating after their lambs, poor creatures. There aren't as many of them as there ought to be. I've lost a lot of sheep in twenty years.

Now, then, let's see . . . Where is she? She must be here. You can't possibly miss her, she's that big. There she is. See her? Under that rowan tree in the corner . . .

What did you say? You don't see her? Of course you do. There she is now, moving towards those two ewes by the hedge. You can't fail to see her unless you're blind.

Are you . . . quite sure? I can't understand it. I can't understand it at all. Dick, Gelli says he's never seen her. My wife says that she's never seen her, that she doesn't know what I'm talking about. Dear God, how am I going to bear it?

Sure, I'm well enough, as far as I know. No, I haven't got a guilty conscience. Why d'you ask? I never harmed a sheep; I've told you, I'm fond of sheep, always have been. I never harmed a *sheep* for certain . . . No, I've never been very happy. I don't really know what happiness is. Does anyone? For me, life has always been something to get through as best I could, hoping each day that the next day would be a little better. A sort of crawling up the slope and slithering back down to the bottom and starting all over again. Isn't that what life is?

Are you sure you don't see her? Yes, of course I can see her. She's watching me now like a stoat, her horns coiled on either side of their head like two snakes. She's black as midnight, she'll bleat in a moment and I'll be sick when I hear her.

I can't understand why none of you see her. But there it is: I understand hardly anything now. One thing I know: I'll never be rid of her. And never is a long time. Isn't it?

Islwyn Ffowc Ellis (1924 -)
(translated by the author)

Llanrhaiadr ym Mochnant

I cannot omit mention of an excursion made to Llanrhaiadr ym Mochnant . . . The church is seated in Denbighshire, dedicated to St Dogvan, son of Brychan. Dr William Morgan, who first translated the Bible into Welsh, was its vicar. He was rewarded by Queen Elizabeth with the bishoprick of Llandaff, in 1595, and was removed to that of St Asaph in 1601, where he died September 10th, 1604 and was interred at the cathedral.

The facetious but learned preacher Dr South was the last rector of the parish. On his dicease, the rectorial tithes were appropriated by act of parliament to the maintenance of the choir and repair of the cathedral church of St Asaph.

I must speak with due respect of the memory of the late worthy vicar, Dr Worthington, to whose hospitable house I was indebted for a seasonable reception, the wet evening which preceded my visit to Pystyll Rhaiadr. This celebrated cataract terminates the precipitous end of a very narrow valley, and, as it were, divides a bold front of the Berwyn mountains. After sliding for some time along a small declivity, it darts down at once two-thirds of the precipice, and, falling on a ledge, has in process of time, worn itself a passage through the rock, and makes a second cataract beneath a noble arch which is has formed; on the slippery summit of which, a daring shepherd will sometimes terrify you with standing. The second fall reaches the bottom and assumes the name of the Rhaiadr, or the cascade. The defect of this noble fall, is the want of wood. When I visited it, the approach was very bad; but that is not only effectually remedied by the late benevolent vicar, but, as I am informed, he has besides erected a cottage as a retreat to the traveller from the fury of the storm.

Thomas Pennant: 'Tours in Wales' (1726-1798)

Berwyn Christmas (1997)

Just south of Oswestry at Llynclys (which is in England) the road to Welshpool turns away from a junction of surprising Border spaciousness, with wide grassy borders, a half-timbered hostelry, and what used to be an old-fashioned iron signpost with 'Llanrhaeadr-ym-Mochnant 13m' painted in black. That was the entrance to my world.

Close by, to the east, over Wat's Dyke, are Morton, Maesbury Marsh, Knockin, and beyond them, some ten miles, Shrewsbury. Its accent, its burr, its deep, slow, landed inflexions, lay over its hinterland to the west, stretching through Llynclys, to Llangedwyn up the Tanat Valley, to Llanrhaeadr-ym-Mochnant.

Only yards into Wales here behind Llangedwyn the luminous Owain Glyndŵr had his court in Sycharth in 1400. There is vigour, and concentration. The Tanat is born in the heart of the Berwyn mountains, behind Pennant Melangell, where the effigies in the small stone church speak of the story of the hare and the metamorphosis of humans, an echo of a mysterious past. The Tanat valley drives like a broken arrow into the Welsh mass. At its head, like a huge upheld arm, is the waterfall. In Llanrhaeadr, take Ffordd y Pistyll, follow the single-track road, blindly twisting westwards, through Commins and Tyn-y-Wern. Step over the last ridge and before you is the vertical silver streak of water falling over an easterly edge of the Berwyns. It drops in a peaty, frothing, pool; through a bridge of rock. Beside it is a farmhouse yet not a farmhouse, with a miniature grandness, its projecting roof supported by old timber pillars. Here, in this narrow end of our valley, foxes were hunted on Boxing Day and I saw the brown streak, the banging of guns echoing against the rocks, the whiskered tail and the never-before smell of the dead fox laid on the road-verge.

The village was stuck in the valley like a stopper in a bottle. Not the Tanat valley at that point but the Rhaeadr valley; this river's sparkling waters having flown through the air from the high moors, through the waterfall, descending around a thousand corners to Llanrhaeadr, flowing under the solid wide-arched road-bridge that marked the boundary between Denbighshire and Montgomeryshire, then behind the church in a long curve, under the hanging dark trees, polishing its stony floor, until joining the Tanat, two miles away at Pedair Ffordd.

Just up from the village, set deep in woods, above the fresh waters of the Rhaeadr, was, of all things, a canal. It was man-made, a neat trough, its waters sluggish, its light brown bottom of mud clearly visible on a bright day. It ended at the turbine-house, inside which a huge metal wheel turned. When turning slowly it uttered a low groan but when the flow of water was good it turned with a happy whine. Along a path and over a stile was a field with cows. In the middle of the field was a two-storey building in pale stone. Inside its door one could see rows of dials and switches. All this was the empire of Mr Smith the Electric. When the lights went yellow and dim at home we knew that the turbine was not doing its work; too many leaves in the water, perhaps, or not enough rain. Then, oil lamps would flame into life. But at night, seldom would the wallpaper in the lounge be entirely lit so that the pattern ran all over the room. The picture-rail was stained brown and pictures hung from it from copper clasps. Flex in brown twists hung along it on tacks at Christmas and twirled around the tree in the corner. Mr Smith would call and make these arrangements. Here was a man who had moved large quantities of earth, who made a huge turbine wheel spin on its axis, who had erected wooden poles along the margins of our streets, hung heavy wires, yet there he was, with fairy-lights.

I particularly liked the round ones, but the pointed ones had their charm too. I held the round one in my hand. It was a strange colour, a creamy-white that might be the colour of well-washed sand; it was like the egg of a rare bird, but corrugated. When lit, in the corner of our room, it gave off a yellow light, inadequate according to the science of voltage, but fitting. It was part of the magic of Mr Smith.

In the dining-room, the table was laid. It had an ironed white cloth, the silver cutlery came out of its wooden box under the sideboard once a year for this occasion. Silver holders with crosses at each end were placed at the head of the table, for the carving knife-and-fork. Their bone handles were grasped in my father's safe hands and before the carving there would be a sharpening of the knife on the sharpening-stone, a movement in the air and the sound of flight. The kitchen had been in maximum use. Its open fire and two green-flecked ovens well stoked-up, surrounded by steaming saucepans. Mother, with her navy-blue dress covered with a tall apron, came out of the kitchen carrying the food, and then finally inside the dining-room took off her apron with deliberation. Father's bald head caught the light as he bent over the turkey. Over our full plates we said a short prayer in Welsh: '*Diolch i Dduw am ein bwyd . . .*'

Under our bent heads we mumbled 'Amen' before raising the heavy cutlery.

The night had been exciting. The anticipation for Christmas is like no other; it is marked on the calendar once a year only. I was sent to bed early and I traced the outlines of flowers on the wallpaper unusually briefly before falling asleep. Once there was an interval in my sleep, probably caused by the door opening, and I saw in the gloom the figure of my father enter the room quietly, carrying a pillowcase. He hung it over the wooden base of the bed, its contents with their straight edges catching the moonlight. I knew that out there there were people who loved me – much better than Santa Claus – and I drifted back to a happy sleep.

When Nain and Taid came, there was a full house. They had been brought in our black Austin Twelve car over the moors through Ysbyty Ifan, over the Cob at Porthmadog and along the road which threaded down the edge of the valley above Llangynog. Nain used two sticks to walk and blocked-up the corridor for ages when she moved from room to room. But my frustration at this (*'Nain, fedrai basio . . . ?'*) was tempered by her marvellous smile, and her musical voice which came out of the kitchen where she conversed with my mother. She had a Meirionydd accent and used words foreign to me. 'Da-da' for sweets and *'cyflath'* for treacle-toffee. This was Grandfather's speciality. *'Mae Taid yn 'neud cyflath'* marked a special Christmas-Eve process. The heavy-base saucepan was found and Taid set to work, his Roman nose and well-combed white hair revealed in the light from the back-kitchen window. The brown liquid frothed and bubbled in the pan as he stirred with a wooden spoon. He melted butter before the kitchen fire and used it to grease two or three flat tins. Holding the saucepan with two hands he poured the lava-like substance into their middle until they filled-out the base of the tin, half-an-inch thick. Then the cooling in the pantry; and the waiting. At the right time, he took a small aluminium-coloured hammer and separated the squares. He put a white powder on them, put them in tins with more powder and the tin shaken. In the drawing-room the tin was handed-around. Then the silence and much munching and cheek-bulging and eyes showing approval:

'Ydi'r cyflath yn dda?' had to be answered.

'Mae'r cyflath yn dda iawn.'

That the toffee was excellent marked the quality of Christmas and the quality of family, where my Grandparents stood for ritual and continuity.

When they sat around the Christmas table, with their coloured paper hats on, Taid and Nain were like the King and Queen. She with her elaborate Victorian blouse with its raised shoulders, fine hair, gold-rimmed spectacles, fingers bent with arthritis and bamboo sticks hooked over the back of her chair. Taid with his extraordinary resemblance to David Lloyd George – his hero: his long white hair straight down each side over his ears, dark suit with waistcoat, a bow-tie, silk, usually polka-dotted. He had a flamboyance. He was a deacon at Capel Garth. His gaiety was matched by his gravitas. He made large-scale comments: he pronounced the word 'world' with a serious rolling of R's. He had a shelf-full of books by and about Lloyd George. His conversation was peppered with words from those politics: Asquith, Treaty, First World War, Munitions, Sylvester, Megan. Also constant in him were boxing, and 'The News of the World'. He listened to the radio – a large bakelite box in the living-room with fat buttons for pressing across the bottom. His large ear would be bent to it hours at a time. He insisted on hearing boxing commentaries. As he picked-up the sounds of fists flying in the ring and the tones of the commentator rising and falling, his head jerked from side-to-side and his white hand jabbed the air. And on Sundays, betweeen Chapel, he would lie on the couch in the drawing-room, away from us, and scan the pages of 'The New of the World' with a studied un-lasciviousness.

His other daughter – Aunty May – lived in Spain. Each Christmas we would get a parcel of presents from them. They were of such style and quality as I had never seen. There was usually a leather item and/or a tie for my brother and myself. The leather was a wallet, beautifully made, flexible and fine-stitched. The tie was silk, long (much too long), thick, in colours of red and yellow. These items entered our utilitarian world like tokens from a place with much greater style and status, of sun, theatre, romance.

Around us, the shoulders of the hills pressed in upon our village. At Christmas it is as if the year holds its breath and, forgetting the tempo of everyday life, its regular Fridays and Mondays, slowly exhales, giving an unexpected day or two of quiet detachment. In 1946 we had it really: snow and snow and snow until the landscape above the sunken Llan was like the moon, white and flat with hedges buried and only the tops of telegraph poles showing. Outside my window, the snow filled the tiny street. It was awesome. Rooks cawed with fury, and the scraping of shovels against stone continued for weeks. You could hear the thump of branches, laden, falling off the trees. And when the thaw and the Spring came, the swifts built their hanging pockets of mud as usual under the broad eaves of our home and the veins of frost that lay over the stones in the river Rhaeadr allowed again the river to sing its way along. It still does.

John Idris Jones (1938 –)

The Legend of Melangell

The pretty legend of Melangell, the patroness of hares, is well known. One day the Prince of Powys chased a hare, which took refuge under the robe of the virgin Melangell, who was engaged in deep devotion. The hare boldly faced the hounds, and the dogs retired to a distance howling, and they could not be induced to seize their prey. The Prince gave to God and Melangell a piece of land to be henceforth a sanctuary. The legend of the hare and the saint is represented in carved wood on the gallery of the church at Pennant. Formerly it belonged to the screen. Hares were once called in the parish of Pennant Melangell Wyn Melangell, or St Marcella's lambs. Until the last century no one in the parish would kill a hare, and it was believed that if anyone cried out when a hare was being pursued, 'God and St Monacella be with thee', it would escape.

Elias Owen: 'Welsh Folklore' (1887)

A Cure for the Shingles

The charming of the shingles was more prevalent in Llanrhaiadr-ym-Mochnant than in any other part of Montgomeryshire. A certain amount of penance was to be done by the sufferer, who was to go to the charmer in the morning fasting, and he was also to be fasting. The mode of cure was simple – the charmer breathed gently on the inflamed part, and then followed a series of little spittings upon and around it. A few visits to the charmer, or sometimes a single one, was sufficient to effect a cure.

Elias Owen: 'Welsh Folklore' (1887)

The Welsh Marches

High the vanes of Shrewsbury gleam
Islanded in Severn stream;
The bridges from the steepled crest
Cross the water east and west.

The flag of morn in conqueror's state
Enters at the English gate:
The vanquished eve, as night prevails,
Bleeds upon the road to Wales.

Ages since the vanquished bled
Round my mother's marriage-bed;
There the ravens feasted far
About the open house of war:

When Severn down to Buildwas ran
Coloured with the death of man,
Couched upon her brother's grave
The Saxon got me on the slave.

The sound of fight is silent long
That began the ancient wrong;
Long the voice of tears is still
That wept of old the endless ill.

In my heart it has not died,
The war that sleeps on Severn side;
They cease not fighting, east and west,
On the marches of my breast.

Here the truceless armies yet
Trample, rolled in blood and sweat;
They kill and kill and never die;
And I think that each is I.

None will part us, none undo
The knot that makes one flesh of two,
Sick with hatred, sick with pain,
Strangling – When shall we be slain?

When shall I be dead and rid
Of the wrong my father did?
How long, how long, till spade and hearse
Put to sleep my mother's curse?

A.E. Housman: 'The Shropshire Lad' (1859-1936)

This poem was written as a response to A.E. Housman's poem. *Amwythig, Henffordd* and *Caer* are Shrewsbury, Hereford and Chester.

Guilty

The border towns are black and white
and peaceful seeming to the sight,
although the stones below the mud
are stained dark red with blood.

In border towns which violence built
there's commerce now of *Sais* and Celt,
false fair-day friends who sell and buy
in *Amwythig, Henffordd, Caer*.

You guilty cities, hear this song:
the stones recall the ancient wrong,
so let your prayers be lifted high,
Amwythig, Henffordd, Caer.

Grahame Davies (1997) Translated by the poet

Debatable Land

Robert Roberts was a cleric and scholar who came from Llanddewi in North Wales. He spent some time in Australia and it was there that he wrote his autobiography, a highly readable account of life in nineteenth century Wales. Here he paints an appealing picture of the village of Castle Caereinion.

> It was situated in a pleasant glen, fertile and well-wooded, opening out into the great valley of the Severn. Offa's Dyke could be traced a mile or two to the east-ward, and the line of demarcation between English and Welsh ran through the parish. The lower division was entirely English, and the upper Welsh; while the village situated about the centre was a sort of Debatable Land. Both languages were known pretty generally, especially by the elder folk, though English was mostly spoken: as to the children, they used English exclusively. And in external features also the country partook of the characteristics of both countries: on the one hand we had a rich, fat valley, thoroughly English in its look of abundance and comfort; on the other, there was a Welsh succession of hills and dales, less rich but very pleasing to look at. On the English side the houses were mostly of brick, red, square, and rather ugly, but the huge ricks, sleek cattle, and blooming orchards took off much of the barrenness. In the Welsh division the houses were built in that most picturesque of styles, with frames of oak, the interstices being filled up with lath and plaster. The poorest thatched cottage had its garden, well filled with fruit trees; the poverty that the richest land is not totally exempt from, was well hidden beneath a mask of picturesqueness, and one might well forget for a time that it had any existence. Coming as I did from a part of the country very uninviting to the eye, the beauty of Castle Caereinion was more striking than it would have been to one familiar with a richer landscape: to me it had all the beauty of Carmel and Sharon combined.

Robert Roberts:
'The Life and Opinions of a Wandering Scholar' (1834-1885)

Welshpool

More popular than poetry are those books which record a town's recent past through old photographs. Welshpool is no exception. Here's one of a procession for Queen Victoria's Diamond Jubilee in June 1897, the children with hats and ladies with black umbrellas shading their complexion from the sun, waved on by Union Jacks. Here's another of Broad Street in the 1950's. It's nearly mid-day on the familiar Town Hall clock, people caught shopping between W.H. Smith and Boots the Chemist.

In the late fifties we lived in Birmingham where my father taught history. My memories are faded pictures of catching buses home from the city; Mam coming home from hospital with a baby sister; learning to read with Dick, Dora, Nip and Fluff.

We moved to Welshpool in 1961. I crossed Broad Street each morning, glanced up at the Town Hall clock and hurried along to Berriew Road Junior School, satchel bouncing on my back. For two first language pupils in our class, Welsh lessons were in the Headmaster's study. Under a high Victorian window and behind a large wooden table, I sat entranced by the Headmaster's dramatic renderings of Pwyll and Pryderi's adventures to strange lands.

Welshpool is an anglicised market town often referred to as the Gateway to Wales. In the Dream of Rhonabwy, one of seven other tales of the *Mabinogion*, Arthur and his knights were to be seen encamped along the river Severn near Welshpool, probably the battle at nearby Buttington in 893. Henry Tudor is also reputed to have camped outside Welshpool on his way to the Battle of Bosworth in 1485. Every summer we were invaded by queues of cars and caravans heading for the coast from the Midlands. Most winters after snow and heavy rain we were besieged by the river, cut-off by road as the brown flood-water plundered low-lying farms and houses.

Across the valley stood Long Mountain, a green ridge that looked down on the town like those watchers in the iron-age hill fort of Beacon Ring or those on Offa's Dyke which crosses the high lonely skyline. Most mornings as I walked down to the High School it would catch my eye, its familiar pattern of fields and woods brooding under cloud or beaming in early sun, mist lingering along the valley and the school's playing fields.

Huw Jones in an article in 'Poetry Wales' (1997)

The Dream of Rhonabwy

In the collection of medieval stories The Mabinogion the one concerning the dream of Rhonabwy is rooted in the area around Welshpool.

Set during the time when Madawc ruled much of Powys, it begins with an account of a search for his missing brother Iorwerth. Iorwerth felt slighted by Madawc's possession of land and decided to resort to violent revenge by murder, destruction and the taking of prisoners.

One of the army of men under Madawc's command is Rhonabwy, and during the search for the villainous brother he and two other men seek refreshment at the home of Heilyr Goch, but are detained overnight by a fierce storm. Rhobanwy falls asleep on a yellow calf-skin and in a dream is transported to King Arthur's encampment on an island on the Severn.

> As soon as sleep had come upon his eyes, it seemed to him that he was journeying with his companions across the plain of Argyngroeg, and he thought that he went towards Rhyd y Groes on the Severn. As he journeyed, he heard a mighty noise, the like whereof heard he never before; and looking behind him, he beheld a youth with yellow curling hair, and with his beard newly trimmed, mounted on a chestnut horse, whereof the legs were grey from the top of the forelegs, and from the bend of the hindlegs downwards. And the rider wore a coat of yellow satin sewn with green silk, and on his thigh was a gold-hilted sword, with a scabbard of new leather of Cordova, belted with the skin of the deer, and clasped with gold. And over this was a scarf of yellow satin wrought with green silk, the borders whereof were likewise green. And the green of the caparison of the horse, and of his rider, was as green as the leaves of the fir-tree, and the yellow was as yellow as the blossom of the broom. So fierce as the aspect of the night, that fear seized upon them, and they began to flee. And the knight pursued them. And when the horse breathed forth, the men became distant from him, and when he drew in his breath, they were drawn near to him, even to the horse's chest. And when he had overtaken them, they besought his mercy. "You have it gladly," said he; "fear nought". "Ha, chieftain, since thou hast mercy upon me, tell me also who thou art," said Rhonabwy. "I will not conceal my lineage from thee; but by my nickname am I best known." "And wilt thou tell us what thy nickname is?" "I will tell you; it is Iddawc Cordd Prydain." "Ha, chieftain," said Rhonabwy, "why art thou called thus?" "I will tell thee. I was one of the messengers between Arthur and Medrawd his nephew, at the battle of Camlan; and I was then a reckless youth, and through my desire for battle, I kindled strife between them, and stirred up wrath, when I was sent by Arthur the Emperor to reason with Medrawd, and to show him, that he was his foster-father and his uncle, and to seek for peace, lest the sons of the Kings of the Island of Britain, and of the nobles, should be slain. And whereas Arthur charged me with the fairest sayings he could think of, I uttered unto Medrawd the harshest I could devise. And therefore am

I called Iddawc Cordd Prydain, for from this did the battle of Camlan ensue. And three nights before the end of the battle of Camlan I left them, and went to the Llech Las in North Britain to do penance. And there I remained doing penance seven years, and after that I gained pardon."

Then lo! they heard a mighty sound which was much louder than that which they had heard before, and when they looked round towards the sound, they beheld a ruddy youth, without beard or whiskers, noble of mien, and mounted on a stately courser. And from the shoulders and the front of the knees downwards the horse was bay. And upon the man was a sress of red satin wrought with yellow silk, and yellow were the borders of his scarf. And such parts of his apparel and of the trappings of his horse as were yellow, as yellow were they as the blossom of the broom, and such as were red, were as ruddy as the ruddiest blood in the world.

Then, behold the horseman overtook them, and he asked of Iddawc a share of the little men that were with him. "That which is fitting for me to grant I will grant, and thou shalt be a companion to them as I have been." And the horseman went away. "Iddawc," inquired Rhonabwy, "who was that horseman?" "Rhuvawn Pebyr the son of Prince Deorthach."

And they journeyed over the plain of Argyngroeg as far as the ford of Rhyd y Groes on the Severn. And for a mile around the ford on both sides of the road, they saw tents and encampments, and there was the clamour of a mighty host. And they came to the edge of the ford, and there they beheld Arthur sitting on a flat island below the ford.

The Mabinogion, translated by Lady Charlotte Guest

Long Mountain

A steep lane on Long Mountain
climbs beside Offa's earthwork,
twisted roots of an oak tree
leap like a boar from the ditch.
Pheasants in bronze finery
break cover, hint of an age
when borders had no meaning.

Beuno, with land at Berriew,
heard the shout of a huntsman
calling his dogs, – the strange tongue
of Mercian settlers. And there,
the shadow of a sentry
cursing the cold, dreaming of
honey cakes in *Valhalla*.

An arrow of geese returns
to Leighton's frozen marchland,
gods of the dyke hibernate
deep as coins under dark stones.
We are captured on camera,
three generations, our speech
sharpened on the wind's whetstone.

We rest at an iron gate,
behind us the western hills
stained with the sun's royal seal.
We migrate with ease across
borders, carry our culture
in a suitcase, fear pressing
like an ingrowing toenail.

Huw Jones (1997)

On Offa's Dyke

Once a concept, now returned to concept
except where the mounded soil
hints of activity, toil,
scoopings, bendings, craft
of earthwork unknit by wind-work.

Once a long snake, sinuous over the land,
over hill heights, above cwms:
now its disintegrated skin
is ghosted in the ground,
buried in its own earth
yet visible here and there
like the life of Offa, Mercian King.
This, in itself, evidence of him,
hegemony's power, fear –
the tangible remains.

Their truths the walls of history hold:
Hadrian's, Jerusalem's, Berlin's –
humanity walled in, walled out,
a wall for weeping on, a wall for execution;
and all our inner barriers, divisions
numerous as the species of wild growth
embedded in this dyke –
taken by the only natural army.

Gladys Mary Coles from 'Leafburners' (1986)

Offa's Dyke

From 757 to 796 Mercia was ruled by a powerful king named Offa. During his reign the Welsh were driven from the border areas along the Dee and the Severn, and English settlers came to live there and to take over their land. There was a period of bitter fighting as the Welsh made great efforts to expel the English intruders. Finally Offa decided to build a great dyke the whole length of Wales, from the Irish Sea in the North to the Bristol Channel in the South. All along the frontier between Wales and England, the English peasants were ordered by their king to dig a deep ditch along a line marked by his soldiers. The earth from the ditch was thrown up on the English side and used to build a great earthen wall. When the ditch on the Welsh side was deep enough – about six feet or more – the diggers then crossed over to the other side, where they dug a shallow ditch. The earth from this shallow ditch was added to the soil and stones already dug up from the first one. The result was a huge earthen barrier, which stretched like a great snake from Chepstow on the Bristol Channel to Prestatyn on the Irish Sea; or more correctly, perhaps, we should compare it to a number of snakes laid nose to tail along this line, for the dyke is not a continuous structure, and there are several gaps in it. This great wall is known as Offa's Dyke, and in many places, along the border between England and Wales it can still be seen, overgrown with grass and bushes; while the ditches have filled up considerably over the centuries, and are, therefore, shallower than they were in Offa's day.

The fact that the English people who lived along the borders were responsible for building the sections of the dyke in their areas, perhaps explains why the dyke appears to be more solidly and evenly constructed in some places than in others, because some English would be lazier than their neighbours, and their work would be less thorough. The Welsh, too, would certainly not stand idly watching their enemies building this barrier, and in many places the workers may have been harassed by Welsh attacks as they went on with the work of building. In some areas the Welsh were so persistent in their raids that the dyke never became a continuous line. In other places the nature of the ground made it impossible for parts of the dyke to be built, and again in some places a river or a cliff-edge were considered to be enough of an obstacle in themselves.

In Flintshire the English settlers probably found very great difficulty in completing their part of this tremendous task which had been given them by their king, for the remains of the dyke in our county are far less spectacular than they are in Mid-Wales. In some parts of Flintshire it seems to have been very poorly constructed, and in others it does not appear to have been built at all. Local tradition claims that the dyke began on the shore near Gronant, at a place called Uffern, but to-day there is no trace of the great earthwork until we come to the village of Trelawnyd (Newmarket). From Trelawnyd it runs to Llyndu, near Babell, in the parish of Ysceifiog, where there is a gap of about 100 yards. There follows a very small length of the dyke, and then it disappears completely for several miles, reappearing at Treuddyn, near Mold. From Treuddyn it can be followed quite clearly all the way across the county boundary to Adwy'r Clawdd, near Coedpoeth, in Denbighshire.

The object of building this massive ditch and wall construction was to mark the boundary between the territories of Mercia and the lands of the Welsh. It may also have had the additional purpose of forming a defensive rampart to protect the Mercians from Welsh attacks, though it was never continuously manned by soldiers, as was Hadrian's Wall in Roman times. The deep ditch on the Welsh side, followed by the wall, which, from the bottom of the ditch to the top of the dyke, was, normally, between 15 and 20 feet high, could have made a very formidable obstacle to any Welsh forces attacking Mercia. It has been suggested that it was built mainly as an obstacle to cattle raiders, but this, at best, is only a guess and anybody who has had experience of the capacity of cattle for straying would not regard it as a very sensible suggestion. In any case, it would appear to have been rather an unwarranted expenditure of time and labour to build such a structure merely to discourage cattle thieving. The most likely explanation would seem to be that Offa, having had much trouble with the Welsh, built the dyke to be a definite and unmistakable boundary between what he considered to be his own dominions and the lands of the Welsh.

An earlier king of Mercia had tried to build a dyke to divide his lands from those of the Welsh. This was probably King Ethelbald, who reigned between 725 and 750. His dyke, which is known as Wat's Dyke, is a much smaller structure and much shorter, running from Basingwerk in Flintshire, to the River Severn at a point near Welshpool. In pattern it is similar to Offa's Dyke, with a deep ditch on the Welsh side and a shallower one on the east. Wat's Dyke probably marks the first boundary which the Mercians were able to establish between themselves and the Welsh. Offa tried to push the boundaries of his kingdom further west, and built his dyke along the hills to try to obtain a more defensive frontier.

On the eastern side of the dyke in Flintshire a number of Saxon villages appeared. The names of these settlements can be traced in the modern place-names along Deeside, though, to-day, many of them have Welsh forms as a result of Welsh re-conquest in later centuries. Preston, Moston, Axton, Boughton and Soughton, are now called Prestatyn, Mostyn, Acstyn, Bychtyn and Sychtyn. Bagillt and Mertyn were also originally Saxon settlements founded during this period of Saxon conquest. Other Saxon villages have retained their English forms down to our own times – Broughton, near Chester, and Kelsterton, near Connah's Quay.

Towards the end of Offa's reign, the Welsh appear to have made an attempt to recover the land which lay between the dyke and the Dee, and a Welsh tradition has been handed down in folk-tale and music, which tells of a fierce battle fought in 796 on Morfa Rhuddlan between the aged king of Mercia and the Welsh prince, Caradoc of Gwynedd. It ended in a tragic defeat for the Welsh. Caradoc was killed and hundreds of Welsh soldiers lost their lives. The plaintive music of the folk song 'Morfa Rhuddlan' is a lament for this defeat. Historians today, however, are disinclined to accept the story of this battle because trustworthy evidence for it is lacking.

'Flintshire from Earliest Times to the Act of Union' (1961)
edited by C.R. Williams

The Pennant on the Dyke

The naturalist and antiquary Thomas Pennant was born at Downing Hall at Whitford in Flintshire. He travelled throughout North Wales and wrote a detailed account of the history and topography of the region. When English literary tourists began to arrive in Wales in large numbers in the late eighteenth and early nineteenth centuries it was frequently as a result of having read Pennant's 'Tours in Wales'. He is known to many outside Wales today as the friend and correspondent of the naturalist Gilbert White, the author of 'The Natural History of Selbourne'.

> Offa's ditch extended from the river Wye, along the counties of Hereford and Radnor, into that of Montgomery, where I shall take it up at its entrance into North Wales, at Pwll y Piod, an ale-house on the road between Bishop's-castle and Newtown; from thence it passes northward, near Mellington-hall, near which is an encampment called Caer-din, by Brompton mill, where there is a mount; Linor park near Mountgomery, Forden heath, Nant-cribba, at the foot of an ancient fortress, Layton-hall, and Buttington church. Here it is lost for five miles; the channel of the Severn probably serving for that space as a continuation of this famous boundary; which, just below the conflux of the Bele and the Severn, appears again, and passes by the churches of Llandysilio, and Llanymynech, to the edge of the vast precipitous lime-stone rock in the last parish: from this place it runs by Tref y Clawdd, over the horse-course on Cefn y Bwch, above Oswestry, then above Sellatyn; from whence it descends to the Ceiriog, and thence to Glyn, where there is a large breach, supposed to be the place of interment of the English who fell in the battle of Crogen, hereafter to be mentioned: it then goes by Chirk-castle; and, below Cefn y Wern, crosses the Dee, and the Rhiwabon road near Plas Madoc, forms part of the turnpike road to Wrexham, to Pentre Bychan, where there is a mount; then by Plas Bower to Adwy'r Clawdd, near Minera; by Brymbo, crosses Cegidog river, and through a little valley on the south side of Bryn Yorkyn mountain, to Coed Talwrn and Cae-dwn, a farm near Treuddin chapel, in the parish of Mold (pointing towards the Clwydian hills); beyond which there can no farther traces be discovered.
>
> Cae Dwn, or rather Cae Twn, according to doctor Davies, signifies fractura, than which nothing can be more expressive of the ending of this famous work, which, as I have not long since observed, terminates in a flat cultivated country, on the farm of Cae Twn, near

Treyddyn chapel, in the parish of Mold. The termination is remote from any hill, or place of strength: it is therefore reasonable to imagine, that this mighty attempt was here suddenly interrupted by some cause, of which we must ever remain ignorant.

No reason appears why its course was not continued from sea to sea. It seems probable that Offa imagined that the Clwydian hills, and the deep valley that lies on this side at their base, would serve as a continuance of his prohibitory line: he had carried his arms over most part of Flintshire, and vainly imagined, that his labors would restrain the Cambrian inroads in one part, and his orders prevent any incursions beyond these natural limits, which he had decreed should be the boundaries of his new conquests. The weakness of this great work appeared on the death of Offa: the Welsh, with irresistible fury, despised his toils, and carried their ravages far and wide on the English marches. Superior force often repelled our countrymen. Sanguinary laws were made by the victorious Harold against any that should transgress the limits prescribed by Offa. The Welshman that was found in arms on the Saxon side of the ditch, was to lose his right-hand.

It is observable, that in all parts the ditch is on the Welsh side; and that there are numbers of small artificial mounts, the sites of small forts, in many places along its course. These were garrisoned, and seem intended for the same purposes as the towers in the famous Chinese wall, to watch the motions of the neighbours, and to repel the hostile incursions.

Thomas Pennant (1726-1798) from 'Tours in Wales'

Wat's Dyke

It is remarkable, that Wat's dyke should have been overlooked, or confounded with that of Offa, by all writers, except by Thomas Churchyard the poet, who assigns the object of the work: that the space intervening between the two was free ground, where the Britons and Saxons might meet with safety for all commercial purposes.

Thomas Pennant (1726-1798) from 'Tours in Wales'

Territorial Clashes

Wales was the refuge of the ancient Britons, when they were driven by the Saxons out of England; and there they preserved the ancient blood royal of their kings, their laws and ancient language from the fury of the Saxons . . .

There continued an implacable hatred and wars between the two nations. When William the Conqueror subdued England, he dispossessed the Saxon issue of the crown; he rooted out most of their nobility, and brought in his own people, the Normans: and when he was in quiet possession of the kingdom, the Welsh took no notice of his Conquest over the Saxons; but accounted of it only as a war between two strange nations.

The kings of England often invaded the borders of Wales, and forced the inhabitants to fly to the mountains; and the Welsh, at other times, made diverse inroads over the Severn, and carried great spoils out of England. This so provoked them the kings, that they resolved to make a conquest of Wales; but the roughness of the country, the hills, woods, and bogs, were such a protection that a great army could hardly be brought to annoy them, but were forced to return home with loss, as William Rufus and Henry II, who entered Wales three times with royal armies.

The kings of England, seeing it difficult to make a conquest of Wales by a great army, gave to the lords, and other great men of England, such counties in Wales as they could win from the Welshmen.

By these means many were drawn to bring great armies of Englishmen and Normans into Wales, who conquered many great lorships, which they held as lands purchased by conquest.

The kings of England having built diverse strong towns of garrison on the frontiers of Wales after the conquest; such as Gloucester, Worcester, and Chester . . . That the lords might the better govern the people when subdued, they were suffered to take upon them such perogative and authority as were fit for the quiet government of the country.

Thomas Pennant (1726-1798) 'Tours in Wales'

Captivity

These are the streets of my mind
and the paths of my memory;
the shafts of my subconscious
run through these hills.
Here was a fragile homeland
for the Welsh of the borders.

The barbed wire on the mountain fences
fastened our language to the land;
so the wind could never scatter it.
But there's rust on the metal thorn.

The captivity of the years
has brought me to the new England,
and made into an exile
one who never wanted to change his world.

Grahame Davies (1997) Translated by the poet

Beautiful Shropshire

Shropshire, beautiful in scenery, and rich withal in mineral wealth, has a history which, in its earlier phases at least, is inferior in interest to that of no other county in England. Upon its soil, the last great battle for British independence is said to have been fought; and the extensive remains of British earthworks and fortifications which, in a connected chain, extending over the whole southern and western portions of the county, concentrate in the vast military works, Caer Caradoc and Oswestry, indicate the fierce nature of that struggle which Caractacus made, to stay the declining fate of his country. The ruins of the city of Uriconium or Wroxeter, and of their highway, Watling Street, as well as numerous vestiges of other Roman settlements and roads scattered throughout Shropshire, attest how futile, after all, had been the efforts of the heroic Briton to resist the victorious progress of the Latin invader; whilst, at the same time, the study of these interesting memorials tends to enlarge our acquaintance with the history of our country during that period of nearly 400 years in which it remained subject to the Romans.

After the departure of the Romans came the Saxons, when the history of Shropshire, including Pengwern or Shrewsbury, the capital of the old British Kings of Powis, whose wattled halls the fair-haired heathen fired; the early history of the county of Shropshire, we say, will be found to contribute towards the elucidation of the question as to how the German invaders eventually made themselves masters of England. It was 'Offa the Terrible', of Mercia, who finally annexed Shropshire to the land of the Angles or England; and he it was who, to secure his acquisition, cast up that remarkable entrenchment known as Offa's Dyke. This great earthwork traverses the border for upwards of a hundred miles over mountain and plain, in its course northwards, forming the boundary between Shropshire and Montgomeryshire.

John Corbet Anderson:
'Shropshire: Its Early History and Antiquities' (1864)

The Letter

'Remember to write.' Clic-di-clac, clic-di-clac, clic-di-clac. The train's clattering wheels jangle mam's words in my mind as I sit in the corner and stare unseeing at the rain rushing by.

'Remember to write.'

I'm looking out of the dirty carriage window. The sea flows past in a hurry to get back to Pwllheli, to Llŷn, to Nain, and to Nefyn. God, I'd give a thousand pounds, two thousand, two thousand and dad's Morris car and the cricket book with Don Bradman's picture, to be playing football in Nefyn instread of going away to school. To be able to turn in my own time on Pwllheli platform after seeing someone else off to school, to walk through the wooden barrier, wait for as long as I like near the Wyman's bookstall and see the counter-full of sweets, to buy a Hotspur and the Sporting Record, and then to saunter out into the lovely rain. I'd stand then in the middle of Station Square and start getting really wet, and I'd look up and down Pen Cob like an old farmer before deciding which way to go. Then I'd turn to the left, in no hurry, and wander slowly towards the bridge. I'd stand there for hours and hours in the rain, watching the swans. Old snobs, swans are, pretending they don't know anyone's looking at them. Down there they go swimming round and round like lunatics for ages, their little black feet pumping like train's wheels underneath them. Like a train. Clic-ci-clac, clic-di-clac; remember to write. 'Dear Mam, I don't like school. Please can I come home. At once. Yours in brief . . .'

But it will be ten weeks before I can walk Pen Cob again. Ten weeks. How long is ten weeks? It's almost as long as from this very second to the end of the world, from today to that time Nain talks about when a drunken man kicked the policeman's hat in Llanllyfni fair, it's like as-it-was-in-the-beginning-is-now'n-for-ever-shall-be-world-without-end-amen. Nobody can see to the far end of ten weeks. It's altogether too long for anyone to think about. I grab my Hotspur and try to read about Cannonball Kidd, who can score a goal from halfway against the best goalie in the world. But it's no use. I can't get interested even in Cannonball Kidd. I can feel a great empty hole in my belly, and I stare out through the window without seeing anything but the drizzle on Pwllheli station. 'Dear Mam. Here's the letter. I've got a pain in my belly. Oh, please can I come home . . .'

I was sitting on the parapet on my bridge when Math came to tell me that I too was going away to school. I didn't understand what that meant to begin with. The bridge wasn't an ordinary bridge then, of course, it was a captain's bridge. My ship was on its way to India and China to see all the treasures of Peru and the little yellow children it talks about in the hymn. When Math rushed pell-mell down past the mill and shouted that he had important news for me, I slunk off to hide on the stone ledge that ran underneath the bridge just above water level, and stayed there still as the stone itself without daring to swallow or to release just one simple tiny breath until I was almost bursting . . .

'Hey, Johnny, I've got big news!'

No answer from me. I move carefully along the ledge, and find a place to sit, then settle down quietly, quietly, with the soles of my feet just tickling the water. I can trail the bottoms of my shoes in the water fine without wetting my feet at all; or only a little bit sometimes. Math changed his tune.

'Captain, sir, I have an important message for the fleet, sir!'

Huh, I say to myself, does he think I was born yesterday? And I sit back in the shadow of the parapet and dream that I'm living in a cave without anyone knowing I'm there, and the whole world far far away.

'Oh, Johnny, come on, I've got something terribly important to tell you.'

What does he have to say, I ponder. Perhaps it isn't bad news after all. Perhaps we'll go for a trip to Pwllheli after lunch. Or farther still. To Bangor to watch the football? What if I miss a trip to Bangor to watch the football?

'All right, kid, if you want to play silly buggers, you won't find out then. Not until you have to.'

I hear Math making a decision, starting off up the hill again. Then I get up suddenly and run along the edge; I don't want to be left alone underneath the bridge; everything is cold and nasty, and the big stones drip green and wet.

'Hello! Math, hello there! Math!'

'Come out of it, you little monkey, so that I can tell you.'

And after I'd climbed, dirty and bedraggled, up the wall and sat beside him on top, I heard the story. I didn't understand at all. Math had been away at school a long time, but that was different. Math was fifteen and a stranger. He didn't really belong in our house.

And now I was going as well. No more walking between the hedges to school. What did 'away' mean? Was it farther than Pwllheli? Perhaps it was as far as Bangor. Math said that the name of the place was Shwsbri, but that meant nothing. It sounded a bit like strawberries, and strawberries could be found in Llaniestyn, if only in Mr Barret's garden. Would it be possible to fish in the pond after being 'away', or to sit on the bridge, or to go to Felin Eithin shop to buy fresh bread and eat all the crust on the way home? Could I play trains in the front room? Clic-di-clac, clic-di-clac. Oh, Mam, I don't want to go to Shwsbri. 'Dear Mam. I don't know where I'll be when you receive this letter. I have jumped off the train. I am going to India because I don't want to go to Shwsbri away to school. Yours truly . . .'

I fling down the Hotspur, stare indignantly at Criccieth station outside, and attack my meat sandwich. It must be hours and hours since I had breakfast.

At Dovey Junction, when I have more or less forgotten the end-product of the journey, and am poking around the platform happily enough, what do I see in the middle of a crowd of people at the far end of the station but a school cap. Exactly the same colour as the sparkling new cap which is safely tucked away in my own pocket. I stand stock still. Then I creep back step by step round the corner to the gents. I stand there for a minute, my heart pumping away and my breath catching in my throat. Another boy going to the same place! Who is he? He looks incredibly clever and beautiful in his cap. I peer around the corner of the gents to look at him. He is standing still in the middle of the platform, with a new, leather case by his side. And what is he doing? Reading a newspaper! The only one I have ever seen reading a newspaper is my father. And my father is old. Do boys read newspapers in Shwsbri? Dear God, what sort of place am I going to?

When the Shwsbri train comes in, I jump smartly into an empty compartment near the back. Please God, I say, don't send that boy into this compartment. But I know perfectly well that it is no good. He arrives soon enough, swaggering his way down the corridor, cap over one ear. And in he comes. After flinging his bag up on the rack overhead and settling himself in a corner, he gives me the once-over, like a farmer at the stock-market.

'I see we're going to the same place,' he says off-handedly, pointing at the corner of my new cap that's peeping stupidly out of my coat pocket.

'I goin' to Shwsbri,' I vounteer.

'Yes, old son, we're all going there on this train,' he says, 'but you and I are going to the same school.'

'Oh. Yes.' There are too many English words chasing each other across his lips for me to follow properly. I can do nothing but sit and stare stupidly at his middle. Oh, Mam, I don't want to go away to old school, where they talk funny and boys with newspapers and no damn anybody speaking Welsh. Diawl, diawl, diawl, I say, leaning heavily on my lonely obscenity, I don't want to go to old school.

'I s'pose you're a new boy,' he offers, after a dreadful, long pause.

'Yes.'

'Mm. Well, you ought to be wearing your cap, you know. It's an offence not to wear your cap.'

'Oh.' I grab my black and yellow cap and stick it on my head. 'Offence?'

'Offence. Crime. Breaking the rules. What's the matter, don't you understand English?'

But the question does not require an answer, and he snuggles up behind his papers and comics to chew sweets and whistle tunelessly from time to time to show that he remembers I'm here. In Welshpool, three others descend on us, everyone laughing madly, thumping backs, pumping hands, and speaking a totally incomprehensible language, with words like 'swishing' and 'brekker' and 'footer' and 'prep'. After they've had their fill of taking each other's caps and kicking each other and flinging cases back and forth, someone notices me.

'What's this, Podge, freshie?'

'Yes,' says the veteran. 'Welshie as well. Can't understand a word of English.'

'Good God.' He gets up and stands in front of me and stares into my face. I can see the blackspots in the end of his nose. By this time, everyone is listening intently. He holds his face within three inches of mine. If I was brave, I would knock this teeth down his throat. If I was like Math or the Saint. But I'm not.

'Welshie are you? Welsh? Welsh?'

'Yes,' I say sadly, 'I am from Pen Llŷn.'

Everyone starts hooting with laughter, rolling around on their seats. The questioner tries again.

'Going to Priestley School are you? School? School?'

'Yes.'

He turns triumphantly to the others.

'Bloody hell, fellers, we'll have some fun with this when we get there. All it can say is yes.'

And everyone starting rolling with laughter once again. I push myself far back into my corner for the remainder of the journey, feel the damn silly wetness in my eyes, and try to think about Cannonball Kidd, about caravans, about Barmouth, about anything but about Mam and Pen Llŷn this morning. Clic-di-clac, clic-di-clac. 'Remember to write a letter.' Clic-di-clac, remember to write.

When the train reaches Shwsbri station, they all forget about me soon enough, and the whole gang rushes out on to the platform, their bags flying in all directions, caps shining new in the rain, everyone talking. On the platform, standing stiff as a poker, there's an ugly woman in a feathered hat, her lips one grim line, and a thin black walking stick in her hand. As each one of them sees her, he stops dead, pulls his cap straight, hauls trousers up, tries to get everything back into line.

'Well.' She looks at them as though she suddenly smells something unpleasant. 'Isn't there anyone else with you?'

Then she sees me standing in my carriage door, cap in hand, and my tie round the back of my neck.

'Oh.' With a come-and-gone smile flashing across her white teeth. 'Here he is. Are you Jones?'

'Yes, missus. My name is Joni Jones.'

'I see. Well, from now on you'll be Jones. Jones J. We don't use names like Johnnie at school, do we? And nice little boys don't say missus, Jones. My name is Miss Darby. Now boys, let's be on our way. We'll all be ready for our tea, I have no doubt.'

And off she goes along the platform, her stick clicking up and down, and her bottom waddling regularly from side to side like a duck's. And everyone follows her quiet as mice, and me following everyone else like Mrs Jones the Post's little terrier dog.

I don't remember much about the next two days, thank God, only an occasional minute here and there. But I know very well that it's all far worse than any nightmare I've ever had about the place before I got here. And I had plenty of those. Everyone in this Priestley looks old and very experienced and talks a mouthful of English. The teachers have never heard of Wales, I don't think, and the cabbage is tough as string and black and green like watercress, and the bed is hard as sleeping on the floor, and the headmaster teaches something called Latin in a room with iron bars across the windows. Every night before going to bed I go to the lavatory to cry quietly and then go back to that old cold barn where everyone is pretending to sleep, and waiting to bait the Welshie.

On Sunday, we are all gathered together in the Latin room with a piece of paper and a small square envelope each, and the head tells us to write a letter home to say we are all right, have arrived safe and have had enough to eat. Well, I grab my brand new fountain-pen, and start to write my letter.

Dear Mum and Dad,
I hope you are O.K. like me. I have arrived safe. The food is quite good and the school is quite nice. I am looking forward to the holidays. Remember me to Spot and to Llyn y Felin.

This in brief,
Joni.

R. Gerallt Jones (1934 –)
Translated from the Welsh by the author)

Illustrious Forebears

Edward Herbert of Cherbury was a Shropshire born philosopher and historian. His father was sheriff of Montgomeryshire. His *Autobiography* creates a vivid picture of the events of his period, as well as providing us with insights into his personality.

> My grandfather was noted to be a great enemy to the outlaws and thieves of his time, who robbed in great numbers in the mountains in Montgomeryshire, for the suppressing of whom he went often both day and night to the places where they were; concerning which, though many particulars have been told me, I shall mention one only. Some outlaws being lodged in an alehouse upon the hills of Llandinam, my grandfather and a few servants coming to apprehend them, the principal outlaw shot an arrow against my grandfather, which stuck in the pummel of his saddle; whereupon my grandfather coming up to him with his sword in his hand, and taking him prisoner, he shewed him the said arrow, bidding him look what he had done, whereof the outlaw was no farther sensible than to say he was sorry that he left his better bow at home, which he conceived would have carried his shot to his body; but the outlaw being brought to justice, suffered for it. My grandfather's power was so great in the country, that diverse ancestors of the better families now in Montgomeryshire were his servants, and raised by him. He delighted also much in hospitality, as having a very long table twice covered every meal with the best meats that could be gotten, and a very great family. It was an ordinary saying in the country at that time, when they saw any fowl rise, 'Fly where thou wilt, thou wilt light at Blackhall', which was a low building, but of great capacity, my grandfather erected in his age; his father and himself in former times having lived in Montgomery Castle. Notwithstanding yet these expenses at home, he brought up his children well, married his daughters to the better sort of persons near him, and bringing up his younger sons at the university; from whence his son Matthew went to the Low Country wars, and after some time spent there, came home, and lived in the country at Dolguog, upon a house and fair living, which my grandfather bestowed upon him. His son also, Charles Herbert, after he had passed some time in the Low Countries, likewise returned home, and was after married to an inheritrix, whose eldest son, called Sir Edward Herbert, Knight, is the king's Attorney-General. His son George, who was of New College in Oxford, was very learned, and of a pious life, died in a middle age of a dropsy.

Notwithstanding all which occasions of expense, my grandfather purchased much lands without doing anything yet unjustly or hardly, as may be collected by an offer I have publicly made divers times, having given my bailiff in charge to proclaim to the country, that if any lands were gotten by evil means, or so much as hardly, they should be compounded for or restored again; but to this day, never any man yet complained to me in this kind. He died at the age of four-score or thereabouts, and was buried in Montgomery church, without having any monument made for him, which yet for my father is there set up in a fair manner.

My great-grandfather, Sir Richard Herbert, was steward in the time of King Henry the Eighth, of the lordships and marches of North Wales, East Wales and Cardiganshire, and had power, in a marshal law, to execute offenders; in the using thereof he was so just, that he acquired to himself a singular reputation, as may appear upon the records of that time, kept in the Paper-Chamber at Whitehall, some touch whereof I have made in my History of Henry the Eighth; of him I can say little more than that he likewise was a great suppressor of rebels, thieves, and outlaws, and that he was just and conscionable; for if a false or cruel person had that power committed to his hands, he would have raised a great fortune out of it, whereof he left little, save what his father gave him, unto posterity. He lieth buried likewise in Montgomery; the upper monument of the two placed in the chancel being erected for him.

Lord Herbert of Cherbury (1583-1648) from his 'Autobiography'

Shrewsbury

The Towne three parts, stands in a valley loe,
Three gates there are, through which you needes must pass
As tò the height of Towne the people goe:
So Castle seemes, as twere a looking glasse,
To looke through all, and hold them all in awe,
Treangle wise, the gates and Towne doth drawe:
But Castle hill spyes out each streate so plaine,
As though an eye on them did still remaine.

In midst of Towne, fower Parrish Churches are,
Full nere and close, together note that right:
The vewe farre of, is wondrous straunge and rare,
For they doe seeme a true love knot to sight:
They stand on hill, as nature wrought a Seate
To place them fower, in stately beautie greate:
As men devout to buyld these works tooke care,
So in these daies these Temples famous are.

Thomas Churchyard (1520-1604) from 'The Worthiness of Wales'

Seeking Respite

12th September, 1774. We left Shrewsbury and set forward to Lord Sandys, where, however, we could not arrive for our tackle broke and our horses tired, and we sought shelter at a little Inn five miles short of our destination. Here, however, we were more pleasantly accommodated than at any of the larger towns, and here we staid till noon the next day, before we thought of going forward. This (12th) September has been very uncomfortable. We breakfasted with Dr Adams, a Clergyman of Shrewsbury, whose welcome, and whose breakfast, and whose conversation were so cold that I was most impatient of delay. When we got further it rained pitiably, and we walked up a steep hill they called Wenlock Edge till our feet were very wet and dirty. The evening made matters worse, but the little Inn at Hartlebury, where all was better than expectation, comforted and refreshed us. Queeney has caught cold again.

Hesta Lynch Piozzi (1741-1821):
Diary of a Tour Through North Wales (1774)

The Sad Fate of Cadman

In the wall near the west door of St Mary's Church (Shrewsbury) is a tablet, bearing the following inscription:

> 'Let this small monument record the name
> Of Cadman, and to future times proclaim,
> How by'n attempt to fly from this high spire,
> Across the Sabrine stream, he did acquire
> His fatal end. 'Twas not for want of skill
> Or courage to perform the task he fell:
> No, no, a faulty cord being drawn too tight,
> Hurried his soul on high to take her flight,
> Which bid the body here below, good night.'
>
> *Feb. 2, 1739. Aged 28*

On Candlemas Day, 1739, a man named Robert Cadman attempted to slide down a rope, from St Mary's spire, which is more than 200 feet high. One end was fastened to the window nearest the vane, and the other to a tree in the Gay. The following handbill had been issued:

'That the famous Robert Cadman intends to fly off St Mary's steeple over the River Severn, on Saturday next, flying up and down, firing off two Pistols, and acting several diverting Tricks and Trades upon the Rope, which will be very diverting to the Spectators.'

Before beginning the descent, he found the rope was too tight, and gave a signal for it to be slackened, but this was misunderstood by the persons below, who made it tighter still, and as the unfortunate man was passing the Dominican Friary, it snapped, and he fell with great force, near the gateway in St Mary's Water Lane. The weather was very severe at the time, and the ground was frozen, so hard that the body rebounded several feet. Thousands of spectators saw the awful sight, and his wife, who was in the crowd collecting money, threw away her gains and rushed to the spot. Some verses on the event, published in the *Gentleman's Magazine*, February, 1740, relate that:

> 'The gazing town was shocked at the rebound
> Of shattered bone that rattle on the ground;
> The broken cord rolls on in various turns,
> Smokes in the whirl, and as it runs it burns.'

It is said that Cadman was a native of Shrewsbury, but this is not certain, although people of the name have been inhabitants, and one, at least, was a burgess. If the rope had held good it seems not unlikely that he would have accomplished his task, for he had performed many exploits at the top of the spire.

'Bygones' February 1874

Eccentric Streets

September 5th, 1855 – Yesterday we all of us set forth from Rock Ferry at half-past twelve, and reached Shrewsbury between three and four o'clock, and took up our quarters at the Lion Hotel. We found Shrewsbury situated on an eminence, around which the Severn winds, making a peninsula of it, quite densely covered by the town. The streets ascend, and curve about, and intersect each other with the customary irregularity of these old English towns, so that it is quite impossible to go directly to any given point, or for a stranger to find his way to a place which he wishes to reach, though, by what seems a singular good fortune, the sought-for place is always offering itself when least expected. On this account I never knew such pleasant walking as in old streets like those of Shrewsbury. And there are passages opening under archways, and winding up between high edifices, very tempting to the explorer, and generally leading to some court, or some queer old range of buildings or piece of architecture, which it would be the greatest pity to miss seeing. There was a delightful want of plan in the laying out of these ancient towns. In fact, they never were laid out at all nor were restrained by any plan whatever, but grew naturally, with streets as eccentric as the pathway of a young child toddling about the floor.

We strolled to a pleasant walk under a range of trees, along the shore of the Severn. It is called the Quarry Walk. The Severn is a pretty river, the largest, I think (unless it be such an estuary as the Mersey), that I have met with in England; that is to say, about a fair stone's-throw across. It is very gentle in its course, and winds along between grassy and sedgy banks, with a good growth of weeds in some part of its current. It has one stately bridge, called the English Bridge, of several arches, and, as we sauntered along the Quarry Walk, we saw a ferry where the boat seemed to be navigated across by means of a rope, stretched from bank to bank of the river. After leaving the Quarry Walk, we passed an old tower of red freestone, the only one remaining of those formerly standing at intervals along the whole course of the town wall; and we also went along what little is now left of the wall itself. And thence, through the irregular streets, which gave no account of themselves, we found our way, I know not how, back to our hotel. It is an uncheerful old hotel, which takes upon itself to be in the best class of English country hotels, and charges the best price; very dark in the lower apartments, pervaded with a musty odour, but provided with a white-neckclothed waiter, who spares no ceremony in serving the joints of mutton.

Nathaniel Hawthorne (1804-1864)
from 'Passages from the English Notebooks'

The Elf

A fair town is Shrewsbury –
The world over
You'll hardly find a fairer,
In its field of clover
And rest-harrow, ringed
By hills where curlews call,
And, drunken from the heather,
Black bees fall.
Poplars, by Severn,
Lean hand in hand,
Like golden girls dancing
In elfland.

Early there come travelling
On market day
Old men and young men
From far away,
With red fruits of the orchard
And dark fruits of the hill,
Dew-fresh garden stuff,
And mushrooms chill,
Honey from the brown skep,
Brown eggs, and posies
Of gillyflowers and Lent lilies
And blush roses.

And sometimes, in a branch of blossom,
Or a lily deep,
An elf comes, plucked with the flower
In her sleep;
Lifts a languid wing, slow and weary,
Veined like a shell;
Listens, with eyes dark and eerie,
To the church bell;
Creeps further within her shelter
Of lilac or lily,
Weaving enchantments,
Laughing stilly.

Neither bells in the steeple
Nor books, old and brown,
Can disenchant the people
In the slumbering town.

Mary Webb (1881-1927)

Recruiting in Shrewsbury

In *The Recruiting Officer* Farquar, one of the leading 17th century dramatists, drew to some extent on his own period in the militia and the play is good humoured, in contrast to the cynicism of Restoration Comedy, which flourished during that period. Here we join Kite as he attempts to swell the ranks at Shrewsbury.

Kite (*making a speech*): If any gentlemen soldiers, or others, have a mind to serve her Majesty, and pull down the French king: if any prentices have severe masters, any children have undutiful parents: if any servants have too little wages, or any husband too much wife: let them repair to the noble Sergeant Kite, at the sign of the Raven in this good town of Shrewsbury and they shall receive present relief and entertainment. Gentlemen, I don't beat my drums here to ensnare or inveigle any man; for you must know, gentlemen, that I am a man of honour. Besides, I don't beat up for common soldiers; no, I list only grenadiers – grenadiers, gentlemen. Pray, gentlemen, observe this cap. This is the cap of honour, it dubs a man a gentleman in the drawing of a trigger; and he that has the good fortune to be born six feet high, was born to be a great man.

Enter PLUME *in a riding habit*

Plume: By the Grenadier March, that should be my drum, and by that shout, it should beat with success. Let me see – (*looking at his watch*) – four o'clock. At ten yesterday morning I left London. A hundred and twenty miles in thirty hours is pretty smart riding, but nothing to the fatigue of recruiting.

Re-enter KITE

Kite: Welcome to Shrewsbury, noble Captain! From the banks of the Danube – to the Severn side, noble Captain, you're welcome!

Plume: A very elegant reception indeed, Mr Kite! I find you are fairly entered into your recruiting strain. Pray, what success?

Kite: I have been here but a week, and I have recruited five.

Plume: Five! Pray what are they?

Kite: I have listed the strong man of Kent, the king of the gypsies, a Scotch pedlar, a scoundrel attorney, and a Welsh parson.

Plume: An attorney! Wert thou mad? List a lawyer? Discharge him, discharge him this minute.

Kite: Why sir?

Plume: Because I will have nobody in my company that can write; a fellow that can write, can draw petitions. I say this minute discharge him.

Kite: And what shall I do with the parson?

Plume: Can he write?

Kite: Hum! He plays rarely upon the fiddle.

Plume: Keep him by all means. But how stands the country affected? Were the people pleased with the news of my coming to town?

Kite: Sir, the mob are so pleased with your honour, and the justices and better sort of people are so delighted with me, that we shall soon do our business.

George Farquar (1678-1707) from 'The Recruiting Officer'

A Neat Town

Montgomery is a neat town, and pleasantly situated; but except St Asaph, it is one of the smallest capital towns in the king's dominions. In the neighbourhood of Welsh Pool, upon a most beautiful eminence, stands Powis castle, formerly called Pool castle, from its vicinity to Welsh Pool; it was built A.D. 1110, by Cadogan ap Bledhyn, who was not long suffered to enjoy it, before he was murdered by his nephew Madoc. Such horrid crimes, however, were so familiar to those days, and so little regarded, that they were frequently committed with impunity, and the offenders might always escape by a fine or dispensation. The castle commands an extensive view of a fertile vale, through which the Severn, yet in its infancy, rolls gently along. The road from thence to Llanvilling is very intricate, and we contrived to lose our way more than once, notwithstanding we have been told it was as straight as an arrow; we wanted about five miles of the latter place, when we met with an honest Cambrian of a very respectable appearance – we did not fail to make some enquiry of him concerning our road; he stopped his horse very politely, and informed us that he was then returning from Llanvilling, the place of his nativity, which he had not seen for more than twenty years before; he added that we should find an excellent inn, and plenty of the best ale in Wales; he then wished us a pleasant walk, assuring us we should meet with princely accommodations, and earnestly recommending the sign of the *goat*, at the same time advising us to make us of his name, for Owen ap Jones ap Evans was as well known as any name in Wales. I relate this little anecdote to you, because I think the character of a people is best delineated by their actions, and their leading features are as completely developed by an action, or an anecdote of themselves, apparently insignificant, as they could possibly be in five hundred philosophical pages.

Joseph Hucks: 'A Pedestrian Tour Through North Wales: 1795'
edited by William Tydeman and Alun R. Jones

A Great Frontier Town

The vales and meadows upon the bank of the Severn, are the best of this country, I had almost said, the only good part of it; some are of the opinion, that, the very water of the Severn, like that of Nile, impregnates the valleys, and when it overflows, leaves a virtue behind it, particularly to itself; and this they say is confirmed, because all the country is so fruitful, wherever this river does overflow, and its water reach. The town, or rather as the natives call it, the city of Montgomery, lies not far from this river, on the outer edge of the country next to Herefordshire. This was, it seems, a great frontier town in the wars between the English and the Welch, and was beautified and fortified by King Henry III; the town is now much decayed.

Daniel Defoe:
'A Tour Through the Whole Island of Great Britain: 1624-1626'

The Last Stand of Caractacas

The western tribes of Britain campaigned bravely against the encroachment of Roman colonisation and Caractacus (Caradoc in Welsh) became the warrior leader of the Ordovices, the tribe who lived in North Wales and the northern border region at that time.

As the Romans were moving south against him he tried to reach his hill fort near what is now Church Stretton – the hill is now known as Caer Caradoc – in order to mastermind his campaign. But he was forced to retreat to another of his forts, between Clun and Knighton, and it was here in 57 AD that the Romans attacked. The Ordovices were outnumbered and outmanoeuvred and following the battle Caractacas' wife and children were captured and taken prisoner. Caractacas himself fled north but was betrayed by another tribe and he also fell into enemy hands. He was then taken to Rome and appeared before Claudius.

This major event in borderland history is related by the Roman writer Tacitus.

> The natural ferocity of the inhabitants was intensified by their belief in the prowess of Caratacus, whose many undefeated battles – and even many victories – had made him pre-eminent among British chieftains. His deficiency in strength was compensated by superior cunning and topographical knowledge. Transferring the war to the country of the Ordovices, he was joined by everyone who found the prospect of a Roman peace alarming. Then Caratacus staked his fate on a battle. He selected a site where numerous factors – notably approaches and escape-routes – helped him and impeded us. On one side there were steep hills. Wherever the gradient was gentler, stones were piled into a kind of rampart. And at his front there was a river without easy crossings. The defences were strongly manned.
>
> The British chieftains went round their men, encouraging and heartening them to be unafraid and optimistic, and offering other stimulants to battle. Caratacus, as he hastened to one point and

another, stressed that this was the day, this the battle, which would either win back their freedom or enslave them for ever. He invoked their ancestors, who by routing Julius Caesar had valorously preserved their present descendants from Roman officials and taxes – and their wives and children from defilement. These exhortations were applauded. Then every man swore by his tribal oath that no enemy weapons would make them yield – and no wounds either.

This eagerness dismayed the Roman commanders disconcerted as he already was by the river-barrier, the fortifications supplementing it, the overhanging cliffs, and the ferocious crowds of defenders at every point. But our soldiers shouted for battle, clamouring that courage could overcome everything; and their colonels spoke to the same effect, to encourage them further.

After a reconnaissance to detect vulnerable and invulnerable points, Ostorious led his enthusiastic soldiers forward. They crossed the river without difficulty, and reached the rampart. But then, in an exchange of missiles, they came off worse in wounds and casualties. However, under a roof of locked shields, the Romans demolished the crude and clumsy stone embankment, and in the subsequent fight at close quarters the natives were driven to the hill-tops. Our troops pursued them closely. While light-armed auxiliaries attacked with javelins, the heavy regular infantry advanced in close formation. The British, unprotected by breastplates or helmets, were thrown into disorder. If they stood up to the auxiliaries they were cut down by the swords and spears of the regulars, and if they faced the latter they succumbed to the auxiliaries' broadswords and pikes. It was a great victory. Caractacus' wife and daughter were captured: his brother surrendered. He himself sought sanctuary with Cartimandua, queen of the Brigantes. But the defeated have no refuge. He was arrested, and handed over to the conquerors.

The war in Britain was in its ninth year. The reputation of Caratacus had spread beyond the islands and through the neighbouring provinces to Italy itself. These people were curious to see the man who had defied our power for so many years. Even at Rome his name meant something! Besides, the emperor's attempts to glorify himself conferred additional glory on Caratacus in defeat. For the people were summoned as though for a fine spectacle, while the Guard stood in arms on the parade ground before their camp. Then there was a march past, with Caratacus' petty vassals, and the decorations and neckchains and spoils of his foreign wars. Next were displayed his brothers, wife, and daughter. Last came the king himself. The others, frightened, degraded themselves by entreaties. But there were no downcast looks or appeals for mercy from Caratacus. On reaching the dais he spoke in these terms.

'Had my lineage and rank been accompanied by only moderate success, I should have come to this city as friend rather than prisoner, and you would not have disdained to ally yourself peacefully with one so nobly born, the ruler of so many nations. As it is, humiliation is my lot, glory yours. I had horses, men, arms, wealth. Are you surprised I am sorry to lose them? If you want to rule the world, does it follow that everyone else welcomes enslavement? If I had surrendered without a blow before being brought before you, neither my downfall nor your triumph would have become famous. If you execute me, they will be forgotten. Spare me, and I shall be an everlasting token of your mercy!'

Claudius responded by pardoning him and his wife and brothers.

Tacitus (AD c.55-c.117): 'The Annals of Ancient Rome'
Translated by Michael Grant

Caractacus: An Inspirational Subject

There have been rival claims over the years about the exact area where this battle occurred. The veteran traveller Pennant was particularly keen to ascertain the truth about this.

The learned editor of *Camden* places it at Gair Ditches, about three miles south of Clun, on the left of the road to Knighton; and gives, as I am informed, a faithful description of the trenches and ramparts. I never saw the place therefore am uncertain on what river it stood, the fords of which were so difficult. No such river is to be seen near the post I ascended; it therefore could not have been the spot on which Caractacus was defeated; yet it is highly probable that it had been a post occupied by him, and that it was named from that circumstance. It has from very remote times been traditionally considered as a strong hold of his; and within no great number of years a society of gentlemen, struck with admiration of his virtue, met annually on the hill to celebrate his name in prose and verse. In one year a gentleman, inspired with the subject, almost instantly delivered a tribute to Caractacus in the following lines:

Brave Caradoc, applauded by thy foes,
What shall thy friends, thy grateful Britons say?
What columns, and what altars rear to fame?

Thrice told five hundred courses of the sun,
Thy age is green, thy laurels freshly bloom.
Yet on thy well-fought hill, whose stony brow
O'erlooks the subject plains, the generous youth
Gladsome repair with annual flow'rs and song,
And festal music, to record thy praise.
Oh for more sparks of thy heroic fire!

Thomas Pennant (1726-1798): 'Tours in Wales

The Coming of the Normans

Then followed one of the Royal journeys into Wales which the Normans inaugurated, journeys undertaken with determination, begun magnificently, but invariably brought to a disastrous close. It was so in this case. Armies melted away before the King. His men craved for a sturdy foe against whom they might contend with vigour, but the sturdy foe viewed them from inaccessible heights, disappeared amidst bogs and woods, then at every fitting moment struck, and not in vain.

Referring to these times, Thierry says: 'It was in the damp and rainy season, and Wales was always one of the most rainy of quarters – the Welsh were invincible. They sent away their women and drove away their flocks into the mountains, broke down the bridge, dug trenches in the pools and exultantly beheld the brilliant cavalry of their enemies sink in the water and mire of their morasses'.

The Normans must have realised to the full the anguish of Ostorius, the Roman, in his Silurian campaign . . .

C. Wilkins: 'Wales Past and Present' (1870)

Sarn

In her novel 'Precious Bane' Mary Webb uses a fictional name for an actual feature of the Shropshire border area. Sarn Mere in the book is, in fact, based on Bomere Pool, about which much folklore is connected. It has been claimed that it is bottomless and that in its depths is a drowned village, the bells of which ring every Christmas Eve.

> . . . there's a discouragement about the place. It may be the water lapping, year in and year out – everywhere you look and listen, water; or the big trees waiting and considering on your right hand and on your left; or the unbreathing quiet of the place, as if it was created but

an hour gone, and not created for us. Or it may be that the soil is very poor and marshy, with little nature or goodness in the grass, which is ever so where reeds and rushes grow in plenty, and the flower of the paigle. Happen you call it cowslip, but we always named it the paigle, or keys of heaven. It was a wonderful thing to see our meadows at Sarn when the cowslip was in blow. Gold-over they were, so that you would think not even an angel's feet were good enough to walk there. You could make a tossy-ball before a thrush had gone over his song twice, for you'd only got to sit down and gather with both hands. Every way you looked, there was nought but gold, saving towards Sarn, where the woods began, and the great stretch of grey water, gleaming and wincing in the sun. Neither woods nor water looked darksome in that fine spring weather, with the leaves coming new, and buds the colour of corn in the birch-tops. Only in our oak wood there was always a look of the back-end of the year, their young leaves being so brown. So there was always a breath of October in our May. But it was a pleasant thing to sit in the meadows and look away to the far hills. The larches spired up in their quick green, and the cowslip gold seemed to get into your heart, and even Sarn Mere was nothing but a blue mist in a yellow mist of birch tops. And there was such a dream on the place that if a wild bee came by, let alone a bumble, it startled you like a shout. If a bee comes in at the window now to my jar of gillyflowers, I can see it all in clear colours, with Plash lying under the sunset, beyond the woods, looking like a jagged piece of bottle glass. Plash Mere was bigger than Sarn, and there wasn't a tree by it, so where there were no hills beyond it you could see the clouds rooted in it on the far side, and I used to think they looked like the white water-lilies that lay round the margins of Sarn half the summer through. There was nothing about Plash that was different from any other lake or pool. There was no troubling of the waters, as at Sarn, nor any village sounding its bells beneath the furthest deeps. It was true, what folks said of Sarn, that there was summat to be felt there.

Mary Webb (1881-1927): 'Precious Bane'

Bomere, Shropshire
(to Mary Webb)

Rings of aged bark
conceal this dark mere,
recipient of life;

muted, the bells in its core
unsounded, drowned
with the village, lost
in the swallowing well
unfathomable as the black hole
of a collapsed star.

Linked trees hold
the spell:
tall lichened alchemists
distilling a special silence,
permitting particular sounds.

Listen! You might hear
the breath of time

whispered in the sipping
of the mere, liquid lips
incessant
to the dipped boughs;
echoed in rooks' raw cries,
contractions of pathos
answered by the bittern
or a solitary heron
objectively fashioning
its reflection;

and ever the hint
of leaf music,
soundless sigh of roots,
mashy moist of earth
becoming mud,
dispersing.

Gladys Mary Coles from 'Leafburners' (1986)

Edwardian Colonisation

Having returned from Palestine, Edward I determined to carry out the ambitious project of annexing Wales to England. With this object in view, he summoned Llewellyn to meet him at Shrewsbury, and do him homage there. The brave Welsh prince, however, was in no hurry to comply with the English monarch's order, when Edward peremptorily summoned him to Westminster. As Llewellyn still continued refractory, he was condemned as a rebel, and military operations were commenced forthwith against him. Regardless of the inconvenience to which he put his subjects, and in violation of the terms of Magna Charta, which direct that the Court of Common Pleas was always to sit in the same place, in order to convince Llewellyn of his determination not to give up the contest until he had gained his end, Edward I now transferred the seat of government to Shrewsbury. 'A.D. 1277. In the fortnight after Easter,' says the contemporary chronicler, 'the king withdrew from Westminster, and hastened towards Wales with all the military force of the kingdom of England, taking with him his barons of the exchequer, and his justices of the king's bench, as far as Shrewsbury, who remained there some time, hearing suits according to the customs of the kingdom of England. Therefore the Welsh, fearing the arrival of the king and his army, fled to their accustomed refuge of Snowdon.' That Edward I was in person at Shrewsbury in the autumn of that year, we know from certain writs which he expedited for the conveyance of stores to the army. He left it on the 16th of October, after which the powerful English king so vigorously pressed his Welsh antagonist, that before the end of the year Llewellyn was forced to yield to the conqueror's hard conditions, and do him homage twice. Having effected a reconciliation with his brother David, impelled by a sense of national ardour, the indignant Welsh prince, however, in 1282, again flew to arms, when Edward, upbraiding him with *ingratitude*, reassembled his army at Shrewsbury, and again removed his courts thither. But death released Llewellyn from the grasp of Edward. The Welsh prince fell near Buelht by the hands of assassins, when, his head having been sent to London, it was derisively encircled by a wreath of ivy, and fixed upon the Tower.

John Corbet Anderson:
'Shropshire: It's Early History and Antiquities' (1864)

In the Border Mountains

From ocean's deep they heaved their scaley hides
More black and solid than the massing clouds
That bar with iron the western light.
Great bones of scarred rock seeming to deride
All weathers, every creature's ravishes.

Now they are blue whales blowing cirrus spume,
With wind-ragged fins; now monumentally calm.
Small birds, dark specks, weave soundlessly a net
In the vast air-space between the mountain sides
In evening flight.
From clouds subtly circling,
The buzzard swoops and drives, makes an affray,
Leans on the wind, soars, and is gone.

The oyster-catcher drops to its stoney nest;
Whining plaintively, peewits, wind-tossed,
Answer the curlew's bubbling call,
Like songs of lost souls; lost, all,
Far beyond the silence and the peace.

The molten stream flares towards the sinking sun,
Which whose huge shadows steal from half the glen.
But towards the sea, in latent golden warmth,
A flowing wind silvers the grasses down,
Where spring wheat's square-cut emeralds, and all
The farms and fields and homesteads lying serene,
Seem so small,
And in the failing light as frail
As pearl-grey shell of abalone.

The light changes, the fields change; people will go.
Created aeons ago, the giant crags remain
It seems for ever; yet each but a nodule
On the earth's rough skin, its creeping crust,
Its creatures wrought in minuscule,
And we some grains of dust.

Margery Lea (1992)

The Devil's Chair

Mary Webb's name is inextricably associated with the border. Her life was a heroic struggle against poverty and illness, but despite these disadvantages she wrote five novels by which she is still remembered today. She also wrote a certain amount of poetry. All her fiction is rooted in the rural landscape of Shropshire and permeated by a sense of the fundamental tragedy of human life; for this reason she has been compared to Thomas Hardy.

A mysterious feature of the topography of the lonely area known as the Stiperstones is the Devil's Chair, a jagged rock formation which stands out sharply and which is associated with a good deal of superstition and folklore.

> Low on the opposite ridge, the larch woods still kept their breathless May freshness, reaching up wistfully toward the gaunt, unchanging heights and the Devil's Chair. Among them the fir-trees reared their tarnished blue-green-sullen, archaic, sentinels of death in a world of immaculate, indomitable youth. A soft, strong wind blew from the west, quick with the year's promise, brimful of meadow and mountain scent. Large clouds continually came up from beyond the Chair, darkened it, swept over the valley, and suddenly disappeared like conjured ghosts as the warm air struck them.
>
> Deborah sat down beneath the signpost, exhausted with a weariness that even the tiny shell-pink fingers, so determinedly fastened on her thumb, could not lift. She looked down at the golden spray of laburnum on her breast, drew in its curious sharp scent, and began to sing in a low voice –
>
> 'Some were sobbing in the gloom
> When we found it, when we found the golden arrow –
> Wand of willow in the secret cwm.'
>
> She looked across at the Devil's Chair – dark and shining as a night-sapphire. It seemed to her that there was no hostility now between the two ranges, between the towering throne and the small white cross. Always before, she had superstitiously regarded the Chair as wholly evil, the Flockmaster's signpost as wholly good. Now she saw good and evil mingled, and felt a slumbering terror in the protecting cross, a hidden beneficence in the inimical stronghold across the valley. Beyond both, behind light and shadow, under pain and joy she felt a presence – too intangible for materialization into words, too mighty to be expressed by any name of man's. Intuitively

she looked at the dogmas she had been taught, and in the fierce light that her experience had lit in her she found them wanting. She had nothing definite to put in their place, only a conception as vague and volatile as light or scent, and without the anaesthetic quality of those creeds that affirm God to be love and goodness only. She was naturally religious, and she felt an almost mystical comfort and rapture in the peace of the Flockmaster's green pastures, and in the presence that dwelt there for her as well as for her father. But away in the black night, among the tomb-like rocks, in the glare of her burnt happiness, she had heard devils laugh, had felt a dark power brood on the crag. Instinct told her that the two visions were one. She was content with the balance of life as she found it, being dimly aware that the terror and the beauty intermingled in something that was more wonderful than beauty.

'The thorn blows late,' she murmured, with the patience of one that has come through tumult and found peace.

Mary Webb (1881-1927): 'The Golden Arrow'

The Wrekin

There was a time I yet remember well,
When oft I've heard the weary reapers tell,
That when at eve the Wreken's top was clear,
Serene and bright the morning would appear,
But when dark clouds his summit should deform,
The day succeeding ever brought a storm:
And many an hour, by murm'ring brook or rill,
I've pensive mark'd the distant Wreken hill,
What time the ev'ning sun declin'd to rest,
And ruddy streaks have ting'd the peaceful west;
Then homeward have I bent my lonely way,
Musing, prophetic, on the coming day.

C.B. Ash (1814)

Thomas Churchyard enjoyed a colourful life as a soldier and subsequently as a courtier in the service of Queen Elizabeth. He was never more than a minor poet, although his work resurfaces in anthologies today from time to time.

Ludlow

The Towne doth stand most part upon an Hill,
Built well and fayre, with streates both large and wide:
The houses such, where straungers lodge at will.
As long as there the Councell lists abide,
Both fine and cleane the streates are all throughout,
With Condits cleere, and wholesome water springs:
And who that lists to walke the towne about,
Shall finde therein some rare and pleasant things:
But chiefly there the ayre so sweete you have,
As in no place ye can no better crave.

Two Bayliefes rules, one yeere the Towne throughout,
Twelve Aldermen they have therein likewise:
Who doth beare sway, as turne doth come about,
Who chosen are, by oth and auncient guise.
Good lawes they have, and open place to pleade,
In ample sort, for right and Justice sake:
A Preacher too, that dayly there doth reade,
A Schoolemaster, that doth good schollers make.
And for the Queere, are boyes brought up to sing,
And to serve God, and doe none other thing.

Thomas Churchyard (1520-1604)

Old-World Charm

Few English towns are more full, even to-day, of old-world charm than Ludlow. Its history has twice been written at length by men of Shropshire birth, one a Ludlow townsman. In the sixteenth century it had its poet Thomas Churchyard, who did his best, though with indifferent success, to describe in fitting verse the town and church and castle.

Ludow, was certainly well fitted to be the Council of the marches' meeting place: it lies high on a knoll girt by the river Teme, in a position easy of defence and yet accessible. It was noted, as

Churchyard says, for the healthfulness of its air, a matter of much importance in days when the plague was a dreaded visitant to towns of any size. The history of Ludlow is closely interwoven with that of the Welsh Marches. According to Camden, the castle was built by Roger of Montgomery, first Earl of Shrewsbury, and forfeited to the Crown by the attainder of Robert of Bellême. It was granted by Henry I to one Fulk de Dinan, who was succeeded by his son, Joce de Dinan, between whom and Sir Hugh de Mortimer raged a feud of the true Border type. Sir Joce got possession of his enemy and detained him in prison till he should pay a ransom of three thousand silver marks, as well as all his plate, horses, and birds. The tower where Mortimer was confined is the loftiest in the third ward of the castle, and still bears his name. In Sir Henry Sydney's Presidency it was used for the keeping of the Council records. Nowadays it serves as a storehouse for the rifles of the Ludlow volunteers, who are drilled in the castle grounds.

Caroline Skeel: 'The Council of the Marches of Wales' (1904)

An Extraordinary Court

Among the extraordinary Courts of the Tudor and Stuart periods special interest attaches to the 'Court of the Council in the Dominion and Principality of Wales, and the Marches of the same'. Its history, extending over more than two centuries, throws much light on methods of government, and also on the social condition of the people within its jurisdiction. The Court was a means of ensuring order in districts long vexed by war, faction, and unpunished crime. It did something to render the union of England and Wales advantageous to both countries; and in spite of many faults, it may be regarded as a fairly successful attempt to grapple with difficulties, the origin of which lay far back in the past. From a purely constitutional point of view it deserves closer study than it has hitherto received. Its relations with the Privy Council, the Star Chamber, and the various local authorities, illustrate that development of both central and local government which especially characterizes the England of the Tudors. In the constitutional struggle of the seventeenth century the Court occupied some place, owing to its conflicts with the Common Law Courts respecting jurisdiction, and its use as an instrument of personal government. Even after its partial abolition by the Long Parliament in 1641, it continued to some extent up to the outbreak of the Civil War; it was revived at the Restoration, and was not finally abolished till the first year of the reign of William and Mary.

Much of what has just been said would apply with equal – indeed, with greater – force to other extraordinary Courts, especially to the Star Chamber. But in one respect the Council of the Marches has an advantage over even that great tribunal – namely, in its associations with some of the most famous names of the sixteenth and seventeenth centuries. Of those who actually presided over the Council the most distinguished are Bishop Rowland Lee and Sir Henry Sydney; but many other notable persons were in some way or other connected with its work. Several of these were of royal blood, as Prince Edward, afterwards Edward V; Prince Arthur, Henry VII's eldest and short-lived son; and the Princess Mary, who passed the happiest years, doubtless, of her life on the Welsh Border. Others were statesmen, such as Lord Burleigh, whose extant memoranda show the minute care with which he supervised the Council's work. Others, again, were lawyers, such as Sir Thomas Englefield in Lee's time, William Gerard a generation later, and Bacon himself, who argued strongly in favour of the Council's jurisdiction over the four Border counties. Lastly, with the Council are linked the names of Milton, Butler, and Baxter. Milton's Comus was acted in the Great Hall of Ludlow Castle, to celebrate the Earl of Bridgewater's entry on his office as Lord President. Butler wrote his Hudibras while steward of the castle and secretary to the Earl of Carbery, and Richard Baxter, in his autobiography, gives a vivid description of Ludlow town as he knew it, full of needy suitors and grasping clerks.

To understand the conditions under which the Council existed, it is necessary to go back four centuries earlier than the date of its institution – to the time when the Norman barons found in the piecemeal conquest of Wales an outlet for the independence sternly denied them in England. Collision between the Welsh and Normans was inevitable; the latter were simply following out the policy which the English Harold had begun. Four years after Senlac, Chester fell and the completion of the conquest of England was the beginning of the conquest of Wales. This was not undertaken by the Norman kings; they had neither time nor inclination for warfare in the rugged mountainous country, where success was doubtful and plunder scarce. The Conqueror was content to plant along the Welsh Border a line of castles for protection against invasion. In them were placed men who, with their Norman instinct for fighting and plunder, might be trusted to conquer Wales for their own profit. The task would be hard enough, he thought, to prevent them from growing over-powerful as against himself.

One of the most noteworthy points in the history of the Council in the Marches is its relation to the various cities and towns in which its meetings were held. Chief among these was, of course, Ludlow; but there were many others, and from their archives much information as to the Council's movements and proceedings can be drawn. The most frequent places of meeting next to Ludlow were Bewdley and Shrewsbury; but the Council at various times held sessions at Hereford, Worcester, Gloucester, Tewkesbury, Hartlebury, Bridgenorth, Oswestry and Wrexham. The list of places visited by that 'stowte travellinge presidente' Bishop Lee would be far longer, for he scoured Wales as well as the Marches in his search for thieves.

Caroline Skeel: 'The Council of the Marches of Wales' (1904)

Sight Seeing

Ludlow is a must for solitary ladies.
They trudge purposefully
From street to street,
Some with cameras,
All with sensibly shod feet,
Absorbed by buildings
Amazed at 'black and white'
And Georgian vistas.

They peer through spectacles.
No smile escapes their lips
Hoping that tea
Will wash away their loneliness,
They make a bargain with a now
That promises a memory,
Carefully preserved,
Of happiness when they were here.

Patricia V. Dawson from 'The Kiln' (1994)

A Chequered History

The chequered history of the Mortimer family in the fourteenth and fifteenth centuries is reflected in the extant notices regarding Ludlow Castle. Roger built a chapel dedicated to St Peter in the 'utter ward', to commemorate his escape from the Tower in 1323. In the fourth year of Edward III's reign he was disgraced, and all his lands were seized to the king's use. His grandson Roger, however, was restored in title and estate, and regained Ludlow among his other possessions. He also had a grandson named Roger, who, on the death of his father, Edmund (husband of the Lady Philippa, daughter of Lionel Duke of Clarence), became the ward of the Earl of Arundel. Roger left a son Edmund, aged six, who became the ward of Henry Prince of Wales, was taken prisoner by Owen Glendower, served in France, and died as Lord-Lieutenant of Ireland in the twenty-fourth year of his age. His cousin Richard, Duke of York (son of his sister Anne), became his heir, and thus Ludlow came to take a leading part in the Wars of the Roses. Here the Duke of York mustered the army which melted away in the so-called Rout of Ludford Bridge. The town was left a prey to the king's soldiers, and was pillaged and burnt. As a compensation for losses sustained in the wars, it received a renewal of its charter from Edward IV, and it seems to have enjoyed special favour during the reigns of the Yorkist kings.

The Castle of Ludlow formed one of the line of fortresses extending from Richard's castle along Corve-dale. The extent to which the Welsh Border was fortified in mediaeval times may be seen by a list of castles drawn up in the earlier years of Henry III. Herefordshire contained nineteen and Shropshire six. One line stretched from Monmouth to Radnor; another skirted the Roman road from Hereford to Shropshire; another, including Knighton, Clun and Bishop's Castle, defended the Welsh Border on the north-west, and the fourth was that of which Ludlow formed one link.

Caroline Skeel: 'The Council in the Welsh Marches' (1904)

Hereford

The Streets like Lanes did seem
Not pav'd with Stones, but green,
Which with red Clay did partly mixt appear;
'Twas Holy Ground of great Esteem;
The Spring's choice Liveries did wear
Of verdant Grass that grew between
The purling Streams.
Which golden Beams
Of Light did varnish, coming from the Sun,
By which to distant Realms was Service don.

Thomas Traherne (1636-1674) from 'Christendom'

A Friend of Human Kind

Earlier in this selection we encountered Joseph Hucks, who travelled through North Wales and parts of the border region accompanied by Samuel Taylor Coleridge. In the passage below he quotes in full a complete poem which Coleridge wrote on the tour. This is concerned with the Man of Ross.

> We slept at the King's Arms at Ross, which was formerly the habitation of that celebrated character who usually goes by the name of the 'Man of Ross'. He was truly a friend to the human kind. He gave his wordly goods, as far as they would go, to the unfortunate; and his best wishes and unqualified compassion to all; his memory is still revered, and his loss still lamented. I cannot omit sending you a few lines which my fellow traveller scribbled upon a window shutter, unlike the general style of composition which such places abound with:
>
> 'Richer than misers o'er their countless hoards,
> Nobler than kings or king-polluted lords;
> Here dwelt the Man of Ross. O traveller hear,
> Departed merit claims the rev'rend tear;
> Friend to the friendless, to the sick man health,
> With generous joy he viewed his modest wealth;
> He heard the widow's heav'n-breath'd prayer of praise,
> He markd the shelter'd orphan's tearful gaze;
> And o'er the dowried virgins snowy cheek,
> Bade bridal love suffuse its blushes meek.

If'neath this roof thy wine cheer'd moments pass,
Fill to the good man's name one grateful glass,
To higher zest shall mem'ry wake thy soul,
And virtue mingle in the ennobled bowl.
But if like me thro' life's distressful scene,
Lonely and sad thy pilgrimage hath been,
And if thy breast with heart-sick anguish fraught,
Thou journeyest onward tempest-tost in thought,
Here cheat thy cares – in generous visions melt,
And dream of goodness thou hast never felt.'

Joseph Hucks: 'A Pedestrian Tour through North Wales: 1795'
Edited by William Tydeman and Alun R. Jones

Ode to the Man of Ross

Rise, honest Muse! and sing the Man of Ross:
Pleas'd Vaga echoes thro' her winding bounds,
And rapid Severn hoarse applause resounds.
Who hung with woods yon mountain's sultry brow?
From the dry rock who bade the waters flow?
Not to the skies in useless columns tost,
Or in proud falls magnificently lost,
But clear and artless, pouring thro' the plain
Health to the sick, and solace to the swain.
Whose Cause-way parts the vale with shady rows?
Whose Seats the weary Traveller repose?
Who taught that heav'n directed spire to rise?
The Man of Ross, each lisping babe replies.
Behold the Market-place with poor o'erspread.
The Man of Ross divides the weekly bread.
Behold yon Alms-house, neat, but void of state,
Where age and want sit smiling at the gate.
Him portion'd maids, apprentic'd orphans bless,
The young who labour, and the old who rest.
Is any sick? The Man of Ross relieves,
Prescribes, attends, the med'cine makes and gives.
Is there a variance? enter but his door,
Balk'd are the Courts, and contest is no more.
Despairing Quacks with curses fled the place,
And vile Attornies, now an useless race.

Alexander Pope (1688-1744) from 'Of the Use of Riches'

An Old Fashioned Town

Old Hall.
Thursday, Nov. 15.

We came this morning from Bollitree to *Ross Market*, and, thence, to this place. Ross is an old-fashioned town; but it is very beautifully situated, and if there is little of *finery* in the appearance of the inhabitants, there is also little of *misery*. It is a good, plain country town, or settlement of tradesmen, whose business is that of supplying the wants of the cultivators of the soil. It presents to us nothing of rascality and roguishness of look, which you see on almost every visage in the borough-towns, not excepting the visages of the women. I can tell a borough-town from another upon my entrance into it by the nasty, cunning, leering, designing look of the people; a look between that of a bad (for *some* are good) Methodist parson and that of a pick-pocket. I remember, and I never shall forget, the horrid looks of the villains in Devonshire and Cornwall. Some people say, 'Oh, *poor fellows*! It is not *their* fault.' No? Whose fault is it, then? The miscreants who bribe them? True, that these deserve the halter (and some of them may have it yet); but are not the takers of the bribes *equally* guilty? If we be so very lenient here, pray let us ascribe to the *Devil* all the acts of thieves and robbers: so we do; but we *hang* the thieves and robbers, nevertheless. It is no very unprovoking reflection, that from these sinks of atrocious villainy come a very considerable part of the men to fill places of emolument and trust. What a clog upon a minister to have people, bred in such scenes, forced upon him! And why does this curse continue? However, its natural consequences are before us; and are coming on pretty fast upon each other's heels. There are the landlords and farmers in a state of absolute ruin: there is the debt, pulling the nation down like as a stone pulls a dog under water. The system seems to have fairly wound itself up; to have tied itself hand and foot with cords of its own spinning! This is the town to which Pope has given an interest in our minds by his eulogium of the *'Man of Ross'* a portrait of whom is hanging up in the house in which I now am. The market at Ross was very *dull*. No wheat in demand. No buyers. It must *come down*. Lord Liverpool's *remedy*, a bad harvest, has assuredly failed. Fowls 2s. a couple; a goose from 2s. 6d. to 3s.; a turkey from 3s. to 3s. 6d. Let a turkey come down to *a shilling*, as in France, and then we shall soon be to rights.

William Cobbett: 'Rural Rides' (1830)
(1763-1835)

A Prospect of Radnor

We were now on the borders of Wales, properly so called for from the windows of Brampton-Castle, you have a fair prospect into the county of Radnor, which is, as it were, under its walls; nay, even this whole county of Hereford was if we may believe antiquity, a part of Wales, and was so esteemed for many ages. The people of this county too, boast that they were a part of the ancient Silures, who for so many ages withstood the Roman arms, and who could never be entirely conquered. But that's an affair quite beyond my enquiry. I observed they are a diligent and laborious people, chiefly addicted to husbandry, and they boast, perhaps not without reason, that they have the finest wool, and the best hops, and the richest cider in all Britain.

One would hardly expect so pleasant, and fruitful a country as this, so near the barren mountains of Wales; but 'tis certain that not any of our southern counties, the neighbourhood of London excepted, comes up to the fertility of this county.

Daniel Defoe:
'A Tour Through the Whole Island of Great Britain 1624-1626'

Down the Magical Marches

John Moore is primarily known as a novelist who wrote of rural life in his native county of Gloucestershire. 'Tramping Through Wales' was a very early work in which he offers us his sometimes tongue-in-cheek impressions of Welsh people and places. Here we find him at the end of his journey.

I worked my way – slowly because of my still-swollen ankle – down the magical Marches, through Hereford and Ross and Gloucester, to my own country-side. I took my time, and followed the obstreperous promptings of my own whim. I attended a horse-fair and was only deterred from buying a grey hunter by the sudden realisation that I had no money. I tickled two half-pound trout in a carefully-preserved stream and left them with a note upon the keeper's doorstep. I played darts and skittles in various inns and pothouses. I asked for gin-and-bitters at one wayside hostelry and was given a pint of beer, which I drank unsuspectingly because I thought it was not worth while correcting the landlord's mistake; thus I tested by accident the physiological effects of drinking a pint of bitter with a double gin in it. At that same inn I met a Welshman who was so intoxicated that his only and original answer to all questions was 'Yes, by damn, no!'

I fished and swam in the Wye, followed the otterhounds up a Border stream, played a game of village cricket, and rode a borrowed pony at a gymkhana. And thus desultorily I came back into England.

It was a fine red sunset when I crossed the Welsh border. I was walking down from the hills into a country-side which I knew well, and for which I had a curious sentimental affection, since it was the scene of my first novel. The little haycock hills, the red sandstone quarries, the hopyards, the silver Wye! I was only nineteen when I wrote that first book. Almost all the ideals and beliefs I had then have gone the way of thistledown when the first autumn winds catch it. For four years the gales of disillusion have blown me hither and thither. Now would I, if I could, turn back the clock's hands and be as I was at nineteen? For I was certainly happier then, and I may – who knows? – have been wiser. Yet I cannot read that book to-day without wanting to destroy it.

The crimson sunset faded over Wales. The mountains were black as night already. Soon the darkness would fall over the dark land behind me, over the companies of towering crags, the thundering waters, the slate-grey towns, the little ugly chapels on the hill-sides . . . I looked back, and saw a single long cloud twisted above the sunset and flushed with its last glow, the Red Dragon which Merlin saw springing out of the hills into the night-sky and rearing angry head and bloody claws above its foe.

The crimson faded, the sky became egg-shell blue. I looked down into the English valley before me, where still, in the deepening dusk, the corncrake challenged the mowing-machine.

John Moore (1907-1967): 'Tramping Through Wales'

Llanthony

I

Llanthony! an ungenial clime,
And the broad wing of restless Time,
Have rudely swept thy massy walls
And rockt thy abbots in their palls.
I loved thee by thy streams of yore,
By distant streams I love thee more;
For never is the heart so true
As bidding what we love adieu.

II

Along Llanthony's ruin'd aisles we walk'd
And woods then pathless, over verdant hill
And ruddy mountain, and aside the stream
Of sparkling Hondy. Just at close of day
There by the comet's light we saw the fox
Rush from the alders, nor relax in speed
Until he trod the pathway of his sires
Under the hoary crag of Comioy.

Walter Savage Landor (1775-1864) from 'Fiosolan Musings'

A Day with Kilvert

Saturday, 26 February 1870

A lovely warm morning so I set off to walk over the hills to Colva, taking my luncheon in my pocket, half a dozen biscuits, two apples and a small flask of wine. Took also a pocket book and opera glasses. Went on up the Green Lane. Very hot walking. At the Green Lane Cottage found Mrs Jones and a daughter at home sewing. Price Price sitting half hidden in the chimney corner but alas there was no Abiasula as the last time I was there. Price Price something like his sister Abiasula. A sturdy boy, with a round rosy good-humoured face and big black eyes, volunteered to guide me to Colva Church. So he came out of his chimney corner in the ingle nook and we started at once, accompanied by a grey and black sheepdog puppy. We were out on the open mountain at once. There was the brown withered heather, the elastic turf, the long green ride stretching over the hill like a green ribbon between the dark heather. There was the free fresh fragrant air of the hills, but, oh, for the gipsy lassie with her wild dark eyes under her black hood. As we went down the Fuallt a grouse cock uttered his squirling crow and flew over the crest of the hill. I never heard a grouse crow before. 'What's that bird crying?' I said to the boy. 'A grouse,' he said, adding, 'There he goes over the bank. They be real thick hereabout.'

Tried to get across the swift Arrow (swollen by the junction of the Glasnant just above) by climbing along a rail but we failed and had to go up a meadow till we got above the meeting of the waters, when we crossed the Glasnant on a hurdle laid flat over the stream and then we jumped the Arrow. Up the steep breast of the Reallt to Dol Reallt and along the road to the Wern and Bryntwyn from whence a field path leads to Colva Church. Here Price Price left me after showing me across one field. I asked him to have some bread and cheese and beer at the Sun Inn, Colva, but he would not and could scarcely be prevailed on to take sixpence. Tried the echo in the field against the belfry and west end of the poor humble dear little white-washed church sequestered among its large ancient yews. The echo was very clear, sharp and perfect. Richard Meredith told me of this echo. Mrs Phillips, the landlady of the Sun, was much frightened when I asked for her husband, uneasy and nervous lest I should have come to apprehend him for having been in a row or doing something wrong. But when I said I wanted the words of an old song, she was greatly relieved and said at one, 'Oh I know who you are. You are the gentleman from Clyro'. I laughed and she began to smile. Mrs Phillips took me into the parlour where I sat down, tore a leaf out of my pocket book and wrote with my address a request that Phillips would send me by post:1. the song about our Saviour; 2. the song about Lazarus; 3. the song about King James and the Tinker. Mrs Phillips brought me a pint of excellent light bright beer, some hard sweet home-baked bread, and some hard cheese, carrying the bread and cheese in her arms as she ran in with it, as I was in a hurry to push on.

Reached Clyro just in time to dress for dinner at Cae Mawr. But as I was going out I was sent for to baptize Mrs Jones the jockey's baby opposite and I was only too thankful that it was so near and that I had not to right about face and march back up to the top of Clyro Hill again. The child was said to suffer from convulsions, so I baptized it, but it was probably quite well. The name selected was as far as I could make out Mahalah which Mrs Jones declared to be the name of one of

Cain's wives, on the authority of a book she had read called the Life of Abel. She called her elder girl Thirza, which she says was the name of Cain's other wife. Not a happy allusion.

The Rev. Francis Kilvert (1840-1879) from The Diary

A Beautiful Vale

I have just had a ramble through the town and part of its neighbourhood and feeling still very lively and having nothing to do but my Journal, am resolved to write it up. Our walk from the village at which we dined and bade adieu to our guide (Estraveildra) was not at first very enchanting. It lay over long round hills, part of the chain of the Black Mountains with not a tree on them to enliven appearances but merely flocks of sheep and geese and droves of cattle. After a while, however, i.e. after 9 miles, we descended towards a beautiful vale, the cultivation of which, when compared with what we had left, seemed in the highest possible state. We wound round a hillside for a long distance with this fine and extensive view before us, gradually however leaving it to the left and coming into another part of the country. Notwithstanding the variety, we still wished for Brecknock and enquiring the distance of a countryman when we supposed we were about 4 miles off, were told it was 7. This surprised us but not so much as the man did when, as a sort of payment for the answer he had given our question, he wanted one to his query of 'from where have you come today?' We soon satisfied and left him; when about half a mile on we saw the town before us, and again enquiring its distance were shown it and told not more than 2 miles and a half. This person also enquired from whence we came and when we said from Cwm Neath doubted with extraordinary sagacity that we were born there. We were satisfied with his answer and the appearance of the town and thought they tallied and we laughed at our first informant as an inquisitive ignoramus. After about half an hour's walk when we expected every moment to fall on to the place, we fell on to a milestone 4 miles from it. We were somewhat fagged and this was a mighty depression to the vivacity with which we were involuntarily preparing to enter the town. However, we trudged on in tactiturn sobriety and were not very long after safely housed at the Castle Inn, a formidably handsome place.

After we had taken tea, I rambled out in the town etc. The place looks like a collection of houses of all sorts, sizes and shapes and colours thrown together in the utmost confusion. The market appeared the best thing about it and was apparently very good, but it must be remembered the evening was dark and I was tired, and only a short time there. The environs seem delightful – Now I must go to bed and prepare for tomorrow.

Michael Farraday (1791-1867): 'Michael Farraday in Wales'

Historic Ground

O.M. Edwards was a writer and educationalist who was born at Llanuwchllyn. Together with certain contemporaries he was responsible for a revival of interest in Welsh literature and learning in the early twentieth century. He was also the founder of Urdd y Delyn, a youth movement which predates Urdd Gobaith Cymru.

Some years ago I was in search of a quiet place: I wanted to read Welsh history in seclusion. By the merest chance I was led to Abergavenny. I thought of going further north, but was so charmed by the view from the train at Abergavenny station – the dark clump of trees on the castle hill, and the exquisitely beautiful Vale of Usk beyond it, – that I determined to get out there and then.

It was a hot August day, but the mid-day heat could not give a parched appearance to the scene – with its wealth of flowers and fruit. The only man at the station in that oppressive heat, except the railway officials, was one whose appearance gave no clue whatever to his age. He was of very slight build, with an undying smile on his lean but pleasant face. He smoked a short clay pipe contentedly in the shade, with his legs crossed, in the deepest unconcern about everything. I crossed over to him, and asked him about hotels and lodging houses. He gave me such curious information, for he looked at everything from a queer point of view; and he gave every place he mentioned unstinted praise.

By means of a severe cross-examination I found that he also had rooms to let, and that, of all rooms in the world, they were the rooms that best suited my purpose. They were in the castle at Abergavenny, the very rooms in which the Welsh princes were murdered, from the windows of which I could have seen the Welsh storming parties climbing the steep rock with their ladders had I come seven centuries sooner, and from the windows of which I could now see the lovely valley and rich plains for which so much blood was shed around this castle, and for which such terrible treachery was contrived within its guilty walls.

By the time we had passed through the old town and reached the castle gate, a thunderstorm was rapidly travelling towards us from the mountains through the sultry oppressive air and sending its cooling breath before it over the dust-covered flowers. We passed through the gate into a spacious courtyard, and the trees which bent over it sheltered us from the big raindrops which were now falling on the thirsty land.

My host told me in his usual imperturbable manner that we were now passing over the spot where the betrayed and murdered Welsh princes were buried. We came to an old harpist who sat in solitude in one of the wall corners, – the thunderstorm having frightened all his dancers away. I asked him for *'Pen Rhaw'*and *'Serch Hudol'*; he had not forgotten them though he had left Carnavon half a century since, and his withered fingers seemed to get new life from the thrills of the triple strings.

I found the hostess most motherly; her husband handed me over to her care, and then assumed, if possible, a more unconcerned air than before. The courtroom of the old castle had been turned into a spacious dining room, – and there I found the hostess and her daughter making a picnic party merry in spite of the thunder that rolled over the ruins. The hostess did all the talking; the host smoked calmly, and smiled the smile of perfect inward happiness.

Before very long the picnic party disappeared, the vast room was made tidy, and work for the day was clearly over. Then the host began to talk – in Welsh. He had been born, – how long ago I could not guess, – in Cardiganshire. Of anecdotes and witticisms he had an inexhaustible store, – and he quietly puffed away at the little clay pipe when our laughter was too uproarious for him to proceed. His recitations of some of Evan Harris' sermons were among the best things of their kind I ever heard.

O.M. Edwards (1858-1920) from 'Wales'

The Rescue of Dick Griffiths

I can say little more memorable concerning myself from the year 1611, when I was hurt, until the year of our Lord 1614, than that I past my time sometimes in the court, where (I protest before God) I had more favours than I desired, and sometimes in the country, without any memorable accident, but only that it happened one time going from St Julian's to Abergavenny, in the way to Montgomery Castle, Richard Griffiths, a servant of mine, being come near a bridge over Usk, not far from the town, thought fit to water his horse, but the river being deep and strong in that place where he entered it, he was carried down the stream. My servants that were before me seeing this, cried aloud Dick Griffiths was drowning, which I no sooner heard, but I put spurs to my horse, and coming up to the place, where I saw him as high as his middle in water, leapt into the river a little below him, and swimming up to him, bore him up with one of my hands, and brought him into the middle of the river, where (through God's great providence) was a bank of sand. Coming hither, not without some difficulty, we rested ourselves, and advised whether it were better to return back unto the side from whence we came, or to go on forwards; but Dick Griffiths saying we were sure to swim if we returned back, and that perchance the river might be shallow the other way, I followed his counsel, and putting my horse below him, bore him up in the manner I did formerly, and swimming through the river, brought him safe to the other side. The horse I rode upon I remember cost me £40 and was the same horse which Sir John Ayres hurt under me, and did swim excellently well, carrying me and his back above water; whereas that little nag upon which Richard Griffiths rid, swam so low, that he must needs have drowned, if I had not supported him.

I will tell one history more of this horse, which I bought of my cousin Fowler of the Grange, because it is memorable. I was passing over a bridge not far from Colebrook, which had no barrier on the one side, and a hole in the bridge not far from the middle; my horse, although lusty, yet being very timorous, and seeing besides but very little on the right eye, started so much at the hole, that upon a sudden he had put half his body lengthways over the side of the bridge, and was ready to fall into the river, with his fore-foot and hinder-foot on the right side, when I, foreseeing the danger I was in if I fell down, clapt my left foot, together with the stirrup and spur, flat-long to the left side, and so made him leap upon all fours into the river whence, after some three or four plunges, he brought me to land.

Lord Herbert of Cherbury (1583-1648) from the 'Autobiography'

Sorrowful Reflections

The Danube to the Severn gave
The darken'd heart that beat no more;
They laid him by the pleasant shore,
And in the hearing of the wave.

There twice a day the Severn fills;
The salt sea-water passes by,
And hushes half the babbling Wye,
And makes a silence in the hills.

The Wye is hush'd nor moved along,
And hush'd my deepest grief of all,
When fill'd with tears that cannot fall,
I brim with sorrow drowning song.

The tide flows down, the wave again
Is vocal in its wooded walls;
My deeper anguish also falls,
And I can speak a little then.

Alfred Lord Tennyson (1809-1892) from 'In Memoriam'

The Severn and the Wye

Giraldus Cambrensis, or Gerald of Wales as he is more popularly known, was born in Pembrokeshire in 1146. His chosen ecclesiastical career was impeded by English hostility. He was twice nominated for the bishopric of St David's but rejected each time.

In 1188 he accompanied Archbishop Baldwin of Canterbury on a journey through Wales to attempt to secure support for the third Crusade. He wrote an informative, frequently entertaining, account of their travels and, in doing so, reveals his keen interest in miracles, folklore, and various unusual natural occurences.

The noble river Severn takes its rise from the Ellennith mountains, and flowing by the castles of Shrewsbury and Bridgenorth, through the city of Worcester, and that of Gloucester, celebrated for its iron manufactories, falls into the sea a few miles from the latter place, and gives its name to the Severn Sea. This river was for many years the boundary between Cambria and Loegria, or Wales and England; it was called in British

Hafren, from the daughter of Locrinus, who was drowned in it by her step-mother.

The river Wye rises in the same mountains of Ellennith, and flows by the castles of Hay and Clifford, through the city of Hereford, by the castles of Wilton and Goodrich, through the forest of Dean, abounding with iron and deer, and proceeds to Strigul castle, below which it empties itself into the sea, and forms in modern times the boundary between England and Wales. The Usk does not derive its origin from these mountains, but from those of Cantref Bachan; it flows by the castle of Brecheinoc, or Aberhodni, that is, the fall of the river Hodni into the Usk (for Aber, in the British language, signifies every place where two rivers unite their streams); by the castles of Abergevenni and Usk, through the ancient city of Legions, and discharges itself into the Severn Sea, not far from Newport.

Gerald of Wales (c1146-1223): 'Itinerary Through Wales'
Translated by Richard Colt-Hoare

A Place of Great Antiquity

Between 1724 and 1726 Daniel Defoe travelled throughout the British Isles and his subsequent impressions make interesting reading. Not only do we learn much about the social and commercial life of the period but we are also, at times, given valuable insights into Defoe's personality.

From hence we came at about 8 miles more into Monmouthsire, and to the town of Monmouth. It is an old town situate at the conflux of the Wye and of Munnow, whence the town has its name; it stands in the angle where the rivers join, and has a bridge over each river, and a third over the River Trothy, which comes in just below the other.

This town shows by its reverend face, that it is a place of great antiquity, and by the remains of walls, lines, curtains, and bastions, that it has been very strong, and by its situation that it may be made so again. This place is made famous, by being the native place of one of our most ancient historians Jeoffry of Monmouth. At present 'tis rather a decayed than a flourishing town, yet, it drives a considerable trade with the city of Bristol, by the navigation of the Wye.

Daniel Defoe (1660-1731)
from 'Tour Through the Whole Island of Great Britain'

Tintern Abbey

Five years have past; five summers, with the length
Of five long winters! and again I hear
These waters, rolling from their mountain springs
With a soft inland murmur. – Once again
Do I behold these steep and lofty cliffs,
That on a wild secluded scene impress
Thoughts of more deep seclusion; and connect
The landscape with the quiet of the sky.
The day is come when I again repose
Here, under this dark sycamore, and view
These plots of cottage-ground, these orchard-tufts,
Which at this season, with their unripe fruits,
Are clad in one green hue, and lose themselves
'Mid groves and copses. Once again I see
These hedge-rows, hardly hedge-rows, little lines
Of sportive wood run wild: these pastoral farms,
Green to the very door; and wreaths of smoke
Sent up, in silence, from among the trees!
With some uncertain notice, as might seem
Of vagrant dwellers in the houseless woods,
Or of some Hermit's cave, where by his fire
The Hermit sits alone:
Though absent long
These forms of beauty have not been to me,
As a landscape to a blind man's eye:
But oft, in lonely rooms, and mid the din
Of towns and cities, I have owed to them,
In hours of weariness, sensations sweet,
Felt in the blood, and felt along the heart,
And passing even into my purer mind
With tranquil restoration:- feelings too
Of unremembered pleasure; such, perhaps,
As may have had no trivial influence
On that best portion of a good man's life;
His little, nameless unremembered acts
Of kindness and of love.

William Wordsworth (1770-1850)
from 'Lines composed a few miles above Tintern Abbey'

The City of the Legions

At the castle of Usk, a multitude of persons influenced by the archbishop's sermon, and by the exhortations of the good and worthy William bishop of Landaf, who faithfully accompanied us through his diocese, were signed with the cross; Alexander archdeacon of Bangor acting as interpreter to the Welsh. It is remarkable that many of the most notorious murderers, thieves, and robbers of the neighbourhood were here converted, to the astonishment of the spectators. Passing from thence through Caerleon, and leaving far on our left hand the castle of Monmouth, and the noble forest of Dean, situated on the other side of the Wye and on this side the Severn, and which amply supplies Gloucester with iron and venison, we spent the night at Newport, having crossed the river Usk three times. Caerleon means the city of Legions, Caer, in the British language, signifying a city or camp, for there the Roman legions, sent into this island, were accustomed to winter, and from this circumstance it was styled the city of legions. This city was of undoubted antiquity, and handsomely built of masonry, with courses of bricks, by the Romans. Many vestiges of its former splendour may yet be seen; immense palaces, formerly ornamented with gilded roofs, in imitation of Roman magnificence, inasmuch as they were first raised by the Roman princes, and embellished with splendid buildings; a tower of prodigious size, remarkable hot baths, relics of temples, and theatres, all inclosed within fine walls, parts of which remain standing. You will find on all sides, both within and without the circuit of the walls, subterraneous buildings, aqueducts, underground passages; and what I think worthy of notice, stoves contrived with wonderful art, to transmit the heat insensibly through narrow tubes passing up the side walls.

This city is well situated on the river Usk, navigable to the sea, and adorned with woods and meadows. The Roman ambassadors here received their audience at the court of the great king Arthur; and here also, the archbishop Dubricius ceded his honours to David of Menevia, the metropolitan see being translated from this place to Menevia, according to the prophecy of Merlin Ambrosius: 'Menevia pallio urbis Legionum induetur'. 'Menevia shall be invested with the pall of the city of Legions.'

Gerald of Wales (c1146-1223): 'Itinerary Through Wales'
Translated by Richard Colt-Hoare

An Important Roman Station

I passed through Caer Went, once an important Roman station, and for a long time after the departure of the Romans a celebrated British city, now a poor desolate place consisting of a few old-fashioned houses and a strange-looking dilapidated church. No Welsh is spoken at Caer Went, nor to the east of it, nor indeed for two or three miles before you reach it from the west.

The country between it and Chepstow, from which it is distant about four miles, is delightfully green, but somewhat tame.

Chepstow stands on the lower part of a hill, near to where the beautiful Wye joins the noble Severn. The British name of the place is Aber Wye, or the disemboguement of the Wye. The Saxons gave it the name of Chepstow, which in their language signifies a place where a market is held, because even in the time of the Britons it was the site of a great cheap or market. After the Norman Conquest it became the property of De Clare, one of William's followers, who built near it an enormous castle, which enjoyed considerable celebrity during several centuries from having been the birthplace of Strongbow, the conqueror of Ireland, but which is at present chiefly illustrious from the mention which is made of it in one of the most stirring lyrics of modern times, a piece by Walter Scott, called the 'Norman Horseshoe', commemorative of an expedition made by a De Clare of Chepstow with the view of insulting with the print of his courser's shoe the green meads of Glamorgan . . .

George Borrow (1803-1881): 'Wild Wales' (1862)

Enchanting Scenes

William Wordsworth and his wife Mary enjoyed a happy marriage, and this is evidenced in the following brief letter written during a period when Mary was travelling in the southern border region with friends. She wrote the following letter to her husband.

2-3 June, 1812
Afterwards we hunted out a blind road by the Wye-side to Monmouth which place we reached about 8 o'clock having passed a glorious afternoon – we had tea & then walked about the town as long as we could distinguish one object from another – when we returned to the Inn – indeed my dearest Love, though I was not the least tired with my ride – my pulses were all beating & I so much enjoyed *perfect stillness* & freedom from exertion of any kind that I could not even ask for pen & ink to write to thee – at Ross I had not time as you will

have observed & this morning we were off as soon as breakfast was over – & O William what enchanting scenes have we passed through – but you know it all – only I must say longings to have you by my side have this day been painful to me beyond expression. We coursed the back of the Wye all the way from Monmouth to Tintern Abbey – the river on our left hand – now *close* to us now at the distance of a stone's throw – & now and then we were separated by a part of the wood which hangs over the Margin – I hope you have paced this blind track – for never did a path lead amongst so much loveliness – what divine villages!

Mary Wordsworth

The Perils of Winter Travel

. . . we passed through Chepstow soon after sunset and pushed on, though it grew dark and the untracked snow lay thick on the ground. About eight we reached the Star, a good though small inn, five miles from Chepstow.

It snowed all night. On Wednesday 17th we set out before day but found it bad travelling, there being no path to be seen, neither footstep or man or beast. However, in four or five hours we reached Abergavenney and Brecon before three in the afternoon.

Our landlady here almost forced us to take a guide. And it was extremely well she did, for the snow had so entirely covered the roads that our guide himself mistook the way more than once. So that if he had not been with us we should without doubt have lodged upon the mountains.

John Wesley (1703-1791): 'John Wesley in Wales'
Edited by A.H. Williams

The Journey to Chepstow

Chepstow, December 19th, 1828

As I had gone yesterday by water, I took my way today along the bank of the river to Chepstow. The country retains the same character – rich, deeply-wooded and verdant; but in this part it is enlivened by numerous iron-works, their fires gleaming in red, blue and yellow flames and blazing up through lofty chimneys, where they assume at times the form of huge glowing flowers, when the fire and smoke, pressed down by the weight of the atmosphere, are kept together in a compact motionless mass.

About midway in my journey the country changed, as it did yesterday, into a stern rocky region. In the centre of a deep basin, encompassed by mountains of various forms, we descried immediately above the silver stream the celebrated ruins of Tintern Abbey. It would be difficult to imagine a more favourable situation or a more sublime ruin. The church, which is large, is still almost perfect; only the roof and a few of the pillars are wanting.

From Tintern Abbey the road rises uninterruptedly to a considerable height above the river, which is never wholly out of sight. The country reaches the highest degree of its beauty in three or four miles, at the Duke of Beaufort's villa called the Moss House. Here are delightful paths, which lead in endless windings through wild woods and evergreen thickets, sometimes on the edge of lofty walls of rock, sometimes through caves fashioned by the hand of Nature, or suddenly emerge on open plateaus to the highest point of this chain of hills, called the Wind-cliff, whence you enjoy one of the most extensive and noble views in England.

Piercefield Park, which includes the ridge of hills from Wind-cliff to Chepstow, is therefore without question the finest in England, at least for situation. It possesses all that nature can bestow and, from the bosom of its own tranquil seclusion, a view into the rich country I have described, which receives a lofty interest from a ruin the most sublime – I mean Chepstow Castle. It covers five acres of ground and lies close to the park on the side near the town, though it does not belong to it.

Prince Puckler-Muskau:
'Tour in England, Ireland and France in 1826, 1827, 1828 and 1829'

A Commercial Centre

Lower down upon the Wye stands Chepstow, the sea port for all the towns seated on the Wye and Lug, and where their commerce seems to centre. Here is a noble bridge over the Wye: to this town ships of good burthen may come up, and the tide runs here with the same impetuous current as at Bristol; the flood rising from six fathom, to six and a half at Chepstow Bridge. This is a place of very good trade, as is also Newport, a town of the like import upon the River Uske, a great river, though not so big as Wye, which runs through the centre of the county, and falls also into the Severn Sea.

This county furnishes great quantities of corn for exportation, and the Bristol merchants frequently load ships here, to go to Portugal, and other foreign countries with wheat; considering the mountainous part of the west of this county, 'tis much they should have such good corn, and so much of it to spare; but the eastern side of the county, and the neighbourhood of Herefordshire, supplies them.

Daniel Defoe:
'A Tour Through the Whole Island of Great Britain' (1724-26)

A Chepstow Inn

William Mackepeace Thackeray is best known as the author of 'Vanity Fair' and 'Henry Esmond', but today this nineteenth century novelist has not, like some of his contemporaries, enjoyed a revival. He is revealed here as the vain man he was.

The rain had poured heavily during the first day of our arrival at Chepstow and it was vain to attempt to see any of the beauties of the place; only the writer of this, having indiscreetly scrambled up a hill on the opposite bank of the Wye, had the pleasure of sitting *perdu* under a thickset hedge for full an hour and a half while the rain poured down. As that great author sat under the hedge he had the misfortune to behold an artist, who had been perched upon a nook of the cliff making a drawing of the town, run away dripping. Nature having covered his drawing over with a transparent wash of her own preparing, and presently afterwards the celebrated literary man rising from his shelter, as there was nothing else for it, had the good luck to find (though, to be sure, the good luck might have come a little earlier) that there was refuge hard by in a little alehouse that goes by the pretty name of the *Bonny Thatch*.

At the *Bonny Thatch* was a policeman drying his wet shins at a snug fire, and a pretty little coquette of a landlady's daughter, a pretty maid and a landlady who had been pretty once, nay is for the matter of that at this present writing, there they were all seated in a window shelling peas. To them presently came two ladies wet through though in pattens, who without ceremony began to arrange their garments in a little shed just outside the door, refusing, however, any offers of aid which some kind wags from within made them. An old dog lay asleep by the fire, on which a pot with a piece of bacon was boiling; near the dog on a carved sort of bench that goes along one side of the room an old landlord was similarly dozing. The room was just six feet two inches and three-quarters in height between the beams and about nine feet square – dark, neat, pretty and comfortable. I should have passed the day there with pleasure, for presently came in various characters – a gentleman whose cart stood in the yard and who arrived with a load of coals, a labourer – I am sorry to say tipsy, though at that early hour in the day – an old tramper with an oiled skin hat on which was written *'One of Nelson's veterans'*.

This old tramper, having had to do with brimstone and charcoal in his early life when the two sent forth shots among the French, was now compelled to deal with the former articles in a much more humble though useful shape. He had a little store of matches by which he made believe to get a livelihood, and accepted a sixpence with perfect willingness, uttering at the same time a long string of tabernacular phrases which were by no means too pleasant to hear. Well, the lay preachers of fancy denominations have done this for us, and the most sacred of all names, which a man ought to go down on his knees before he uttered, is bandied about by every prating vagabond with a familiarity that makes one sad to hear.

I should like to have had this fellow out of the conventicle and upon the deck; he had served with Nelson and Collingwood, he said, and afterwards with Admiral Pellew who was made Lord Exmouth (please lay the emphasis on the mouth): but the fact was the landlady, being a person of very genteel turn of mind (indeed as I learned afterwards she had been ladies' maid to a respectable family), would not allow one to remain in the snug little Fieldingian kitchen, but insisted that the gentleman should go and sit in an upstairs room which she usually let to her lodgers. I could not but obey, and there found myself on a damp day looking upon Chepstow Castle, or with the liberty to look at it if I chose; but as the rain was so strong that it was impossible to see it I preferred to read Mr Lockhart's Valerius, which I had the good luck to carry with me. And it is very probable that the reader would have been surprised by an elaborate criticism upon that book (which is full of learning and thought, and of passion and right feeling where the author dares to unlace himself to avow it, and the hero of which may be designated as a most gentlemanlike, Bond Street Christian) – I say that the reader might probably have been charmed at the very next sentence by a criticism upon Valerius, had not the real owner of the lodgings at the *Bonny Thatch* come into

his appartment. It is a very snug and pretty one, but it appears the landlady in her zeal to show what rooms she had quite forgot the laws which make every man's lodging his castle and introduced me to the privacy of another person.
The only reply which the occupier of the room made was to offer me a dinner, and lend a cloak to go home in. May there be many such kind acquaintances for all wayfarers in the wide rainy world!
The girl of the *Bonny Thatch* said that the price of his room and board (I will witness that I saw a most excellent repast consisting of a beefsteak, new potatoes, the very peas that I had the honour to see shelled, and the bacon that had just issued from the very pot before mentioned) – the price of two rooms and board is a guinea weekly. A guinea a week, think of that! At six hours, from London, in the face of a beautiful landscape, in a little quiet shady hedge inn, with the Chepstow town and castle before you, with the Wye running under them, and on the Wye the best salmon that was ever eaten in the world.
A lunch at the *Bonny Thatch*, consisting of cheese, butter, bread and excellent hard cider, costs 4d.
But to return to the salmon. This is without contradiction the most delightful of all the varieties of the fish that I have ever tasted. It is impossible to describe its freshness and beauty. It comes to you with all the dew upon it, as it were. It is almost a shame to put any sauce to it. It is best eaten with a little salt and a slice of bread. It leaves the inner man in an unspeakable state of rapture and ease and comfort. It remains upon the recollection quite gratefully, as some joy which one has experienced and can't forget, something for which one should be thankful always.

William Makepeace Thackeray (1811-1863): 'Cockney Travels' (1842)

Chepstow

He who by land would enter Chepstow town
Must quit his horse and lead him gently down:
The long descent so rugged is and steep
That even post-boys here for safety creep;
The sloping road demands our utmost care –
Hawker when living never galloped here.

Cats with sharp claws and nanny-goats in dread
Descend the shelving street and cautious tread.
What must we men then do to walk secure?
Observe the good old proverb – slow and sure;
For if we careless walk the slippery street
Our prostrate nether-ends the pavement greet;
And paying oft such honour to the stones
Will fix domestic prophets in our bones:
For when old bruises ache, they full as well
As corns and whip-cord change of weather tell.
But though in feat the street the stranger treads,
Within he'll find sure footing and soft beds;
The inns will furnish every want and wish,
For there he'll find good flesh, good fowl, good fish;
And those who on crimp salmon wish to feast,
In great perfection there will find it dressed.
Here is good ale, good cider and good wine
So that like sons of kings we here may dine.
In this snug town good meat and drink abound
But, strange to tell,there cannot here be found
One single inch of horizontal ground:
To social joys folks therefore here incline,
By way of exercise sit down to dine,
Grow plump and rosy, like the god of wine.

If strait the gate and narrow be the way
That leads from earth to realms of endless day,
Then through this town must be the road to heaven,
Whose gate is strait, streets narrow and uneven.
Such is the town of Chepstow, rugged, steep,
But a choice place to revel in, and sleep.

Edward Davies (1718-1789) from 'Chepstow: A Poem'

In The Forest of Dean

Bollitree,
Wednesday, Nov. 14, 1821

Rode to the Forest of Dean, up a very steep hill. The lanes here are between high banks, and, on the sides of the hills, the road is a rock, the water having, long ago, washed all the earth away. Pretty works are, I find, carried on here as is the case in all the other *public forests*! Are these things *always* to be carried on in this way? Here is a domain of thirty thousand acres of the finest timber-land in the world, and with coal-mines endless! Is this *worth nothing*? Cannot each acre yield ten trees a year? Are not these trees worth a pound a piece? Is not the estate worth three or four hundred thousand pounds a year? And does it yield *anything to the public*, to whom it belongs? But it is useless to waste one's breath in this way. We must have a *reform of the Parliament*: without it the whole thing will fall to pieces. The only good purpose that these forests answer is that of furnishing a place of being to labourers' families on their skirts; and here their cottages are very neat, and the people look hearty and well, just as they do round the forests in Hampshire. Every cottage has a pig, or two. These graze in the forest, and, in the fall, eat acorns and beech-nuts and the seed of the ash; for, these last, as well as the others, are very full of oil, and a pig that is put to his shifts will pick the seed very nicely out from the husks. Some of these foresters keep cows, and all of them have bits of ground, cribbed, of course, at different times, from the forest: and to what better use can the ground be put? I saw several wheat stubbles from 40 rods to 10 rods. I asked one man how much wheat he had from about 10 rods. He said more than two bushels. Here is bread for three weeks, or more, perhaps; and a winter's straw for the pig besides. Are these things nothing? The dead limbs and old roots of the forest give *fuel*; and how happy are these people, compared with the poor creatures about Great Bedwin and Cricklade, where they have neither land nor shelter, and where I saw the girls carrying home bean and wheat stubble for fuel! Those countries, always but badly furnished with fuel, the desolating and damnable system of paper-money, by sweeping away small homesteads, and laying ten farms into one, has literally *stripped* of all shelter for the labourer. A farmer, in such cases, has a whole domain in his hands, and this, not only to the manifest injury of the public at large, but in *open violation of positive law*. The poor forger is hanged; but where is the prosecutor of the monopolizing farmer, though the *law* is as clear in the one case as in the other? . . . Down the deep and beautiful valley between Penyard Hill and the hills on the side of the Forest of Dean, there runs a stream of water. On that stream of water there is a *paper-mill*. In that paper-mill there is a set of workmen. That set of workmen do, I am told, *take the Register*, and have taken it for years! It was to these good and sensible men, it is supposed, that the *ringing of the bells* of Weston church, upon my arrival, was to be ascribed; for nobody that I visited had any knowledge of the cause. What a subject for lamentation with corrupt hypocrites! That even on this secluded spot there should be a leaven of common sense!

William Cobbett (1763-1835): 'Rural Rides' (1830)

The Best Ways Into Wales

The best way into Wales is the way you choose, provided that you care. Some may like the sudden modern way of going to sleep at London in a train and remaining asleep on a mountain-side, which has the advantage of being the most expensive and the least surprising way. Some may like to go softly into the land along the Severn, on foot, and going through sheath after sheath of the country, to reach at last the heart of it at peaty Tregaron, or the soul of it on Plynlimmon itself. Or you may go by train at night; and at dawn, on foot, follow a little stream at its own pace and live its fortnight's life from mountain to sea.

Or you may cross the Severn and then the lower Wye, and taking Tredegar and Caerleon alternately, or Rhigws and Landore, or Cardiff and Lantwit, or the Rhondda Valley and the Vale of Neath, and thus sharpening the spirit, as an epicure may sharpen his palate, by opposites, find true Wales everywhere, whether the rivers be ochre and purple with corruption, or still as silver as the fountain dew on the mountain's beard; whether the complexions of the people be pure as those of the young cockle-women of Penclawdd, or as heavily supercribed as those of tin-platers preparing to wash. Or you may get no harm by treading in the footsteps of that warm-blooded antiquarian, Pennant, who wrote at the beginning of his tours in Wales: 'With obdurate valour we sustained our independency . . . against the power of a kingdom more than twelve times larger than Wales: and at length had the glory of falling, when a divided country, beneath the arms of the most wise and most warlike of the English monarchs.' That 'we' may have saved the soul even of an antiquarian.

Edward Thomas (1878-1917) from 'Beautiful Wales'

Other books by the same author:
Visitors' Delight
A Clwyd Anthology
The Teatime Guide (with Pamela Roberts)
The A to Z of North Wales (with Pamela Roberts
The Land of Old Renown
Christmas in Wales